BALM IN GILEAD
And Other Plays

BALM IN GILEAD

And Other Plays

By

LANFORD WILSON

A Dramabook

HILL AND WANG

THE NOONDAY PRESS

New York

To Tanya

ISBN (clothbound edition): 0-8090-2805-0
ISBN (paperback edition): 0-374-52156-5

Library of Congress catalog card number: 65-24711

First Edition September 1965

Noonday Press edition, 1988
Nineteenth printing, 1990

CONTENTS

Balm in Gilead was first presented by Ellen Stewart at the Cafe La Mama Experimental Theater Club, New York City, on January 26, 1965. It was directed by Marshall W. Mason, with the following cast:

JOHN	Marvin Alexander
ERNESTO	Thomas Ambrosio
CARLO	Howard Benson
BABE	Savannah Bentley
RUST	Claris Erickson
BONNIE	Linda Eskenas
FICK	Neil Flanagan
FRANNY	Frank Geraci
DAVID	Gary Gusick
TIG	Paul Kilb
RAKE	John Kramer
MARTIN	Matthew Lewis
BOB	Harry McCormick
FRANK, AL	Jerry Newman
DARLENE	Avra Petrides
DOPEY	Michael Warren Powell
KAY	Barbara Randolph
JOE	Gregory Rozakis
TERRY	Lucy Silvay
ANN	Mary Tahmin
XAVIER	Dennis Tate
STRANGER	Robert Thirkield
TIM	Ronald Willoughby
JUDY	Phoebe Wray

Lighting by Dennis Parichy, assistant director Roderick Nash, Stage Manager Lola Richardson, assistant to the producer Zita Litvanas.

Balm in Gilead was presented by the Steppenwolf Theater Ensemble at the Steppenwolf Theater in Chicago on September 18, 1980. It was directed by John Malkovich, with the following cast:

JOHN	John Mahoney
ERNESTO	Kim Nardelli
CARLO	Paul Jones
BABE	Debra Engle
RUST	Billie Williams
BONNIE	Rondi Reed
FICK	Terry Kinney
FRANNY	Jeff Perry
DAVID	Doug Gould
TIG	William L. Petersen
RAKE	Alan Wilder
MARTIN	Rick Snyder
BOB	Robert Biggs
FRANK	Bill Williams
AL	Michael Moore
DARLENE	Laurie Metcalf
DOPEY	Gary Sinise
KAY	Kathi O'Donnell
JOE	Francis Guinan
TERRY	Michelle Banks
ANN	Glenne Headly
XAVIER	Tom Zanarini
STRANGER	Tom Irwin
TIM	Randy Amov
JUDY	Joan Allen
CHILDREN	Aaron, Dylan, and Greg Kramer

Set and lighting by Kevin Rigdon.

Balm in Gilead was presented by the Circle Repertory Company and the Steppenwolf Theater Ensemble at the Circle Repertory in New York City on May 15, 1984. It was directed by John Malkovich, with the following cast:

JOHN	Paul Butler
ERNESTO	Giancarlo Esposito
CARLO	Lazaro Perez
BABE	Debra Engle
RUST	Billie Neal
BONNIE	Tanya Berezin
FICK	Terry Kinney
FRANNY	Jeff Perry
DAVID	Brian Tarantina
TIG	James McDaniel
RAKE	James Picken, Jr.
MARTIN	Jonathan Hogan
BOB	Bruce McCarty
FRANK	Zane Lasky
AL	Burke Pearson
DARLENE	Laurie Metcalf
DOPEY	Gary Sinise
KAY	Betsy Aidem
JOE	Danton Stone
TERRY	Karen Sederholm
ANN	Glenne Headly
XAVIER	Tom Zanarini
STRANGER	Tom Irwin
TIM	Mick Weber
JUDY	Charlotte Maier
CHILDREN	Adam Davidson, Eben Davidson, Erinnisse Heuer, and Samantha Kostmayer

Set and lighting by Kevin Rigdon. The production then transferred to the Minetta Lane Theatre, where it opened on September 6, 1984.

BALM IN GILEAD

A Play in Two Acts

NOTES

SCENE: An all-night coffee shop and the street corner outside. Upper Broadway, New York City.

The café is represented, or suggested, in the center of a wide, high stage. There are a counter and stools (one unit) and across a wide aisle, a row of booths (one unit). They should be constructed so the actors can raise and move them easily. There is also some indication of an area behind the counter; and a skeletal indication of a front door and large front window.

Actors wander onto the set from both sides and back; they gather in the café and outside, where the street corner would be (downstage left). There is a generally congested feeling inside the café—when it is crowded there are always a few people standing in the aisle. The stage should look open; a general feeling of looseness should be conveyed in the design of the set and the random wandering of people. The confining factor is their number.

Much of the play consists of several simultaneous conversations in various groups with dialogue either overlapping or interlocking. These sections should flow as a whole, without specific focus; they rise and subside and scenes develop from them.

Everything seems to move in a circle. Within the general large pattern the people who spend their nights at the café have separate goals and separate characters but together they constitute a whole, revolving around some common center. They are the riffraff, the bums, the petty thieves, the scum, the lost, the desperate, the dispossessed, the cool; depending on one's attitude there are a hundred names that could describe them. They live within as rigid a frame, with its own definitions, as any other stratum. Their language, their actions, their reading of morality is individual but strict.

3

CHARACTERS

A number of "hoods" (A general term that could cover almost everyone in the play, but defines more specifically the petty thieves, bargainers, hagglers, pimps. They will steal anything from anyone and sell anything including themselves to any man or woman with the money, although they could not be described as homosexuals. Their activities in this area are few and not often mentioned.):

BOB
XAVIER
TIG, *a male prostitute (hustler)*
MARTIN, *a heroin addict*
RAKE, *a hustler*
DOPEY, *a hustler-addict*
ERNESTO, *a hustler—Colombian*

Some are junkies as well, as noted, some are hustlers; definitions overlap. DOPEY is a heroin addict as well as a sometimes-not-too-good hustler. What they are now is not what they will be a month from now. A number of the men have no special classification; they might have part-time jobs at times; they might do a number of things, but are not involved in any specific activity:

TIM
CARLO, *a Colombian*
JOHN, *the waiter-grill man*

A number of the girls are Lesbians; some have boys' nicknames; they might be prostitutes as well:

TERRY
RUST
JUDY

Other characters include:

FICK, *a heroin addict who sometimes provides a background to the rest of the action.*
BABE, *a heroin addict who sits stony silent at the counter through the first half of the play. (When the set is moved, she walks beside it.)*
KAY, *the waitress.*

FRANNY, *an almost transvestite boy—very beautiful, very feminine.*
DAVID, *much like* FRANNY, *not so "lovely."*
BONNIE, *a prostitute.*
ANN, *a prostitute.*
STRANGER, *about thirty-five.*
FRANK, *about fifty-five.*
AL, *a bum, about fifty.*

The production should concentrate on the movement of the whole, slowly focusing on JOE and DARLENE:

JOE, *a New Yorker, typical middle-class metropolitan background. He is twenty-four, good-looking, of average height and build. He has dark hair. He has a guarded reaction to everything and everyone. He speaks clearly.*

DARLENE, *an attractive girl, twenty to twenty-three; recently arrived from Chicago; she speaks with a candid, Midwestern voice that sets her apart from the sound of the rest of the play. She is honest, romantic to a fault, and not at all bright. The actress playing* DARLENE *should be aware that she is supposed to be stupid, and not the sweet, girl-next-door, common-sense-saves-the-day type of ingenue.*

FOUR NEGRO ENTERTAINERS
FOUR CHILDREN

Most of the characters are about twenty-three to thirty years old.

The play covers a week or two just before Halloween. The rock'n'roll song at the beginning and near the end should be accompanied by recording; the round is not accompanied. The pace of the play, except in a few scenes, should be breakneck fast. There is one intermission.

BALM IN GILEAD

ACT ONE

*A noise from a crowd begins and reaches a peak as the curtain rises.
From the wings come four Negro entertainers (two from each side)
who sing a rock'n'roll song with much clapping, dancing, etc. They
are accompanied by a typical clangy, catchy instrumentation. From
far out on the apron they sing to the audience—very animated. As
the song fades out, and they begin to move (still singing) back off
the stage, the noise from the group rises again.*

FICK [*outside the café, to one of the four singers as the song ends.*
FICK *will talk to anything that moves*]. Hey, fellow, buddy; you got
a cigarette? Baby? Hey, fellow—could you—hey, friend? [*They are
moving off.*] Screw it. [*To someone else.*] Hey buddy? [*He wanders
to the street corner group of* DOPEY, ERNESTO, JOE, *and* RAKE.]

BOB [*as one of the singers runs by him he reaches out and grabs his
behind. The crowd in the café notices this and laughs.* BOB *whirls
around to them*]. I never seen a singer yet that was goosey! [*Crowd
laughs.*]

TERRY [*from the café*]. I never seen a nigger yet that was, I know
that!

ERNESTO. Yeah, you watch your mouth! [*He laughs.*]

TIG [*from the café*]. You just watch that, Terry-boy.

JUDY. All right! Come on. If we're going to get goin' in here, get
goin', get that table out of the way, come on; line them up a
little.

A few people straighten the booths into rows.

TIG [*overlapping**]. What are you, some kind of housewife, Judy?

JUDY [*to* DAVID]. You're the housewife, aren't you, sweetheart?

DAVID. You're the fishwife, Judy. Fishwife, Fish. Pheew!

FICK [*on the corner, to* JOE]. Hey, Joe; Joe.

JOE. I'm going in.

DAVID [*to* JUDY]. A better housewife I'd make, sweetheart, than you
ever will.

BONNY [*to* FRANNY *and* DAVID]. You ought to be chased out of the
neighborhood. You clog up the air with a lot of fairy dust. Fairy
dust.

* "Overlapping" will indicate that the speech is started during the preceding
speech.

7

FRANNY [*overlapping*]. Who you calling a name, you truck driver?

FICK [*to* JOE, *overlapping*]. Me too, in a minute; you in with Chuckles like they say? I heard you're going to be tying in with him. If I wasn't, hey, such a junk, you think he'd take me?

BONNY. Who you queers think you are?

DAVID. Who you callin' queer, George!

BOB. Shut up, over there!

JOE [*to* FICK]. He might, you work on it, okay, Fick?

DOPEY. Get lost, Fick.

FICK [*to* JOE]. You know why I will? You know why I'll work on that? Because, hey, one thing Chuckles will give you is a good protection, you know? They hear you're tied in with Chuckles they'll leave you alone, baby.

TERRY [*over** FICK's *speech; she is very drunk*]. All you queens.

JOE [*cutting into* FICK's *speech*]. Okay, Fick, that's enough.

TIG [*at the counter to pay—someone has bumped him*]. Come on, God.

FRANNY [*to* TERRY]. Why don't you shut up before I beat you over your head with your dildo?

TERRY. You trying to say something?

FICK [*to* JOE]. I didn't mean anything by it.

JOE. You just talk too much, baby, you know it?

FICK [*joking*]. You wouldn't get Chuckles after me, would you? Look at me, man, I'm, hell, I'm weak as a kitten.

FRANNY [*over, to* TERRY]. Ah, your mother's a whore——

TERRY. You trying to say something?

TIG [*to* FRANK, *counting his change*]. What the hell are you talking about——

FRANK. Why don't you stop coming in here, you don't——

TIG. What the hell, you're trying to screw——

FRANK [*cutting in*]. Get on out now.

TIG. You trying to cheat me outta four bucks, baby, you can't pull——

FRANK. I never cheat you outta nothing.

TERRY [*over, to* DAVID *and* FRANNY *who are watching* TIG *and* FRANK]. You queers just sit down, take it easy.

TIG. I gave you a five, a five, you son of——

FRANK. You get on out of here.

* "Over" will indicate that the speech is said simultaneously with the preceding speech.

Tig. You want to step outside? You want to step out from behind that counter, baby? You watch it, Frank.

John [*cutting in*]. Come on, Tig, give up, go on out.

Frank. Get out of this place.

Tig [*to* John]. Ah, come on, I gave him a five, man, you know what he's trying.

John. Come on, go on, Tig.

Tig [*leaving café for street corner*]. You wait, Frank; you'll get yours, buddy.

Frank. [*after* Tig *has gone*]. Get on out of here, bum!

Tig [*yelling back heatedly now*]. All right, now, goddammit I'm out, you just shut your mouth, Frank. You stupid bastard.

Frank. You get on, bum!

Tig. Buddy, you're really gonna get it one day, Frank, and I want to be there to watch it. You're gonna get your head split open, dumb bastard.

Fick [*this exchange should begin during the exchange above, cued by* Frank's "*You get on out of here*"]. You wouldn't do something like that, would you, Joe?

Joe. Just don't talk so much. What makes you think I even know Chuckles?

Fick. You're not going to turn him down are you? Something like that?

Joe. We'll see, won't we?

Fick. 'Cause, man, I wouldn't do that, I know that. Course you're a strong guy, I'm weak as a kitten. That's too much of a hassle for me. I'd take some of Chuckles' protection, man; he——[Joe *pushes him away slightly and walks to the café.*] Yeah, well, nice seeing you, buddy; you come around any time. Any time, we'll talk again, babe, okay?

Joe *enters the cafe.*

Note that in production, each group, and there are several of them, must maintain a kind of life of its own. The group on the street corner, for instance, usually Rake, Dopey, Tig, *and* Ernesto, *loiter with nothing much to say. Improvised, unheard conversations may be used. Characters may wander along the street and back, improvise private jokes, or stand perfectly still, waiting. The same goes for groups in the café, such as* Terry, Rust, *and* Judy. *Their lines should come from scenes developed within the situation. Aside from this, it should be mentioned that everyone in the café (with the exception of BABE and FICK) looks up the moment someone enters the café: a kind of reflex "once-over" to evaluate any new opportunity or threat.*

TIM [*at the counter, to* FRANK]. Hey, Frank, could I have a hot tea, okay?

FRANK. Shut up. All you hoodlums.

TIM. What the hell did I say? [*To himself.*] I'm kinna drunk.

FRANK. Just shut up that. Hoodlums. This is a decent place; you guys ruin it for everybody!

DAVID. Why the hell you yelling at him; he hasn't done nothing.

TERRY. Shut up, Frank.

TIM [*over*]. I didn't say anything.

RUST [*running into café*]. Hey, they got Jerry Joe in the can!

BOB. Jerry the fairy?

DAVID. Watch who you're calling names.

RUST. He tried to put the make on a cop.

BOB. They gonna book him?

JOHN [*to himself*]. Dumb fag.

RUST. Whatta you mean? He tried to put the make on a cop. Hell, yes, they'll book him. He had eight bombinos on him! Man, are they hot for that stuff.

General crowd reaction.

FRANK. Come on, knock it off.

KAY. Fry two, John.

FRANK. I'm going now, Johnnie; you take over.

RUST. I wish I'd seen his face!

FRANK [*as* DOPEY *tries to enter the café*]. Now keep out. Come on, you know you don't get served, come on get out. Junkies and dopes and whores——

FRANNY. Who's a whore?

FRANK. ——What kind of a neighborhood is this? I'll go, Johnnie.

BOB [*to* FRANK]. Swinging.

FRANK. I'll swing you, right out of here. *Exits.*]

JOHN. Come on, now, keep it down.

TIM. May I have a tea, please?

BONNIE [*at a booth, reading a check*]. What the hell is this, fifty cents for one Coke, you think this is the Ritz?

JOHN. There's a sign right there, fifty cents minimum at booths; if you don't have it, don't sit there.

BONNIE. Screw it, I'm payin' no fifty cents for one Coke.

KAY [*to* JOHN]. Toast with that.

BOB. Fifty cents you can get a good high.

BONNIE. Gimme a cheese sandwich; hell, if I'm going to spend a fortune. One goddamned Coke.

KAY. And a jack.

DAVID [*cutting in—to* BOB]. Come on up to my room, it won't kill you.

BOB. Knock it off. [*To* ANN.] How much you make tonight, Ann?

ANN. Huh?

DAVID [*joking more than anything*]. Come on up with me, it won't kill you.

BOB. How much scratch? Jack? Tonight?

ANN. None of your damn business. Ask Sammy, you want to know.

TIG [*has wandered back in; he is standing near* ANN]. You still keepin' that bum? What's he do with all that dough?

ANN. He banks it. Or at least he'd better be banking it.

BOB. Yeah, he banks it with Cameron or Chuckles.

ANN. He don't truck with that junk. He'd better not; I'd crack him over the head.

TIG. Feed him bennies you'll keep him limp—he won't go messing around.

KAY [*to* BONNIE]. Whatta you want on the cheese?

ANN. I don't need him limp; limp for five minutes he can limp out in the ever-loving street.

BONNIE. I don't care—Christ.

BOB. Who's name does he bank it in?

TIG. Come on, how much you clear last night?

ANN. Clear? It's all clear; what do you think I do make out an income-tax report?

DAVID [*to* BOB]. You comin' up?

BONNIE. Hey, Kay, make that a cheeseburger.

JOE [*to* ANN]. He keeps at it—I like his drive.

ANN. I like sex drive.

KAY. Make up your mind!

JOE. That's all you ever think about. I'm working now, I tell you.

ANN. You think I don't work? I'll show you my bunions.

JOHN [*to* TERRY]. Whatta you want for a quarter?

Suddenly lights dim into full blink for a second only. Dim on all of café; spot on JOE. *Held for a second only, with no reaction anywhere else.*

KAY. Onions on that?

BOB [*to* ANN]. I got something you could use.

KAY. You want onions on that?

DAVID. Well, are you?

BOB. No, I'm not coming up! Look, I don't dig boys; fags. Understand? Not unless you got a roll on you.

DAVID. Don't knock it till you've tried it.

BOB. I happen to like tits. You got tits?

General laughter.

BONNIE. And another Coke. Put some ice in it this time, okay?

ANN. Come on up, Joe. I won't bite you. Sammy's out.

JOE. I told you I'm a working boy, now.

ANN. Yeah, I'll bet. You pushing your box? Hustling it down to Forty-second?

JOE. Who, me? Not on your life.

KAY [*calling to* JOHN]. All the way.

BONNIE [*to* KAY]. Grilled onions, why not.

JOHN [*to* DAVID *who is leaving*]. You pay?

ANN. You are; I'll bet.

DAVID. Yes, I paid; I paid half an hour ago.

BOB. You get tits, you come back and let me know.

DAVID. You go to hell. Who needs you? [DAVID *leaves café as* MARTIN *enters, almost bumping into him.*] Watch out, for Christ's sake.   *Exits.*]

MARTIN *spots* JOE *from across the café.*

ANN. Come on up, Joe.

MARTIN. Joe, hey!

ANN. Hey, John; give me another coffee. You're getting worse than Frank.

JOHN. Watch your language.

ANN. What'd I say?

MARTIN. Hey, Joe, you got any?

JOHN. You said Frank. [ANN *laughs.*]

JOE. Any what?

MARTIN. You know. Come on.

TIG [*ordering*]. Plain Pepsi.

JOE. What you want with me? I got nothing you want.

ANN [*to* JOE]. You got something I want.

TIG. No ice.

MARTIN. Joe, no kiddin', I gotta. Man, you don't know! Don't play games with me, baby.

JOE. I'm not playing games, Martin.

The quartette have entered café and are standing in back. They harmonize in an off-key improvisation a rock'n'roll song, with some-one using a table for a drum.

BOB. Hey, Tig.

MARTIN. Just one, Joe. I gotta, man. You don't know.

TIG [*to* BOB]. Yeah, what's in it for me, huh?

JOHN [*to* ANN]. You wanted coffee. Cream?

TIM. I think I'm gonna be sick.

JUDY [*to* TIM]. You okay?

MARTIN. Come on, baby.

JOE. Go where you usually go.

JUDY. You want a tomato juice or something?

TIM. God, no.

JOHN. Cream, Ann?

TIM. Okay.

ANN. Black.

JOE. Go where you usually go.

TIM. No I don't, either.

ANN. You got the lousiest service.

MARTIN. I go to Jerry Joe.

BOB [*overhears, turns around, then back*]. Jerry the fairy?

MARTIN. Yeah, well, Jerry the fairy's in the can. In the box, man. Come on, Joe. You got any? I heard you could.

JOE. You go to Jerry Joe? That's a sad turn of events.

TIM. I'm all right.

MARTIN. Don't play with me, baby. What's the matter with you guys, you think as soon as you get a pinch to push you can play games and play big shot with everyone.

JOE. I'm not playing games, Martin. I'm your friend. I don't follow what you're talking about is all. You're not making sense.

MARTIN. Come on, Jerry Joe's in the can.

*Phone rings—*JOHN *goes to answer.*

JOE. Look, Martin. If I was just starting out—I couldn't take on the whole neighborhood, now, could I?

MARTIN. Why not, man; corner the market.

JOHN [*on the phone*]. What?

JOE. Yeah, and get cornered.

FRANNY [*to* TIG]. Have you seen Lilly?

JOHN [*holding the phone*]. Anybody here named Carol?

FRANNY. If that's my husband, tell him I dropped dead   *Exits.*]

ANN. If that's Sammy, tell him I'm turning a trick. [*All laugh.*]
Under the table. [*Laughs.*]

BONNIE. You could do it too.

ANN. If anybody could, honey.

> JOHN *hangs up the phone.*

TIM. Could I have another tea, John.

JOHN. Sure.

> TIG *gets up to leave.*

JOE. Why don't you go somewhere else, come on.

MARTIN. 'Cause I come to you. What the hell's wrong? Come on,
buddy.

TIG [*yelling to* JOHN]. Hey, what time you get off?

JOHN. Seven in the morning.

TIG. Whatta you work, seven to seven?

JOHN. Yeah. Swingin' hours, huh?

TIG. Christ! [*Leaves café for street corner.*]

MARTIN. What's wrong, huh? I come to you.

ERNESTO [*enters the café from the street corner*]. Coffee. Lottsa
cream. No, black. Black. And a chocolate cupcake. How much is
a cake?

JOHN. Twenty-five. Big one's thirty.

ERNESTO. Just the coffee's okay. Black. Black.

ANN. Black.

JOHN. Black.

JOE. Look!

> FICK *enters over* JOE'S *line and begins his long wandering dialogue.*

JOE. Look! Martin, baby.

Sudden dim again. Spot on JOE *and* MARTIN. *Everyone holds their
positions. Stop-motion.* FICK'S *dialogue and movement continue
over the pause as though nothing else were happening.*

Look. . . .
You come back about ten o'clock. And I'll see. Okay?

Spot dims on JOE *and* MARTIN *and then natural lighting resumes.*

JOHN [*fakes a blow to* ERNESTO's *side*]. Come on, I'll show you. Take that. Pow!

ERNESTO [*fake reaction. Sudden violence here, though it is only a kind of horsing around*]. Gad, in the liver—I'll get you for that one . . .

TIG [*on the corner. Slaps someone on the back*]. You're a pal.

ERNESTO [*to* JOHN]. You're a pal!

BOB *leaves café for street corner.*

ANN [*very rapid exchange here. To* ERNESTO]. You're a pal.

MARTIN. You're a pal, Joe! You're great! [*Hesitantly.*] You're sure? [*Starts to go.*] Sure?

JOE. Ten o'clock. I'll see you. Don't go talking to anyone, okay?

MARTIN. You know me, I'm your friend.

JOHN [*to* MARTIN]. Did you pay?

MARTIN. You don't know how cheap you make a fellow look. Asking did he pay. You make people look cheap talking like that. You make people feel cheap talking like that.   Exits.]

FICK [*This dialogue begins in the background of the scene page 14 at* JOE's *first "Look!" Very softly*]. Man, it's getting cold out there, isn't it? Hey, John, fix me up with a coffee, could you? Warm up a little bit, you know what I mean? That's no good, walking around out there dressed like I am in this weather, I mean it isn't cold yet, but it's getting there and I'm not going to be dressed any warmer in another month when it comes. Kid like me. That's no good for you—you know, with alcohol you're not so bad because it's in your blood stream, you know, but with horse like I take you got to watch out 'cause you don't notice the cold and the first thing you know you're sick as a bitch, man, and about all I need is to go into a hospital or something like that and let them start looking me over, you know? That's about like all I need, man. What is it, about October? About the middle of October, huh? Damn it'll be getting really cold before long. You know what I mean?

BOB. Hey, Tig, I got something you'd like I bet. Hey Dopey.

TIG. What?

RUST [*to* KAY]. Miss, could I have a soup?

ANN [*to* JOE]. What are you into now?

TERRY [*to* KAY]. Two, okay? What is it?

DOPEY. Yeah, what?

BOB. I'll bet.

KAY [*to* TERRY]. Bean—lima.

JOE. What do you mean?

ANN. What are you into now?

RUST. Christ. Well, okay.

JOE. Come on, keep it down.

ANN [*standing up*]. Well, I gotta go, if you aren't coming up. You just watch yourself, Joey buddy. [*She pays her bill.*]

KAY. Two soup, Johnnie.

JOE. Dammit, don't worry about me. I know what I'm doing.

FRANNY [*re-enters the café*]. Has anybody seen Red tonight?

ANN *Exits.*]

JOE [*to* FRANNY, *making up for being irritated by* ANN]. Not since last night, baby.

FRANNY [*flat*]. Jerry Joe's in the can. Had about a dozen bombinos on him.

JOE [*to* FRANNY, *irritated suddenly*]. Go get laid, why don't you?

DOPEY [*on the corner; to* RAKE]. I tell you I kicked it.

FRANNY [*to* JOE *over*]. Who's tickling your ass? Be like that, I don't need you. You're working for Chuckles now?

JOE. Mind your own, sweetheart; you live longer.

RAKE. Sure.

JUDY [*to* TERRY]. I'll be back. [*She goes to* TIM.]

DOPEY. No, I did. Yes, I did.

RAKE. Hell you did.

DOPEY. I will, you wait.

TIM. I'm sick. I knew I was.

KAY [*with soup, to* RUST *and* TERRY]. It's hot.

JUDY. You okay?

FRANNY. Chuckles can kiss it, honey; my second husband was a pusher. I don't owe him nothing; he's not my type.

JOE [*getting up*]. Why don't . . .

TERRY [*from the back of the café, regarding* JUDY]. Now she thinks she's some kind of wet nurse.

RUST [*to* TERRY]. One's just like the other.

BOB *and* TIG *enter café from corner.* AL *enters café from offstage.*

JUDY. Hey, Rake. Over here.

RAKE *leaves the corner, enters the café, looks around.*

JOHN [*to* RAKE]. Come on, come on, Rake. We can't serve you. Run
out on checks—go on, back out in the street, Rake. You know
that.

RAKE [*to* JOHN]. Screw you.   *Exits to corner.*]

CARLO [*enters. To* TIM]. Hello.

TIM [*sick*]. Not now, Carlo.

CARLO. *Ernesto, ¿cómo está?*

AL. Give me a coffee, okay? Noisy, ain't it?

KAY. Coffee, okay.

TIM [*gets up*, JUDY *follows him, trying to take him home*]. Damn,
I think I'm sick. None of you are worth a good——

ERNESTO. Carlo.

JUDY. Come on you're drunk as a judge. Come on, let's get you
home or somewhere, okay?

ERNESTO [*to* CARLO]. *¿Qué pasa, Chico?*

TIM. Carlo can hardly speak English even. [*To* JUDY.] Take your
hands. Not worth a damn. [*Staggers forward.*] Take your—dike,
you go with girls. Mess around with your own kind.

TERRY [*over*]. I don't care where she sleeps or who she sleeps with!

JUDY. Come on.

TIM. Take your hands off me, you go with girls. You're a whatsit.
[*Aside to the audience.*] She's a whatsit, without a gizmo.

JUDY. Come on, you're drunk.

TIM. At least I'm drunk on drunk, not on junk like everyone . . .

JUDY. Come on, Tim, you're drunk. You're sick, Timmy.

TIM. I'm *sick*? [*To audience.*] I'm sick? She's a thingamabob!

JUDY. Come on, go on home, Tim.

TIM [*to audience*]. Listen! [*Aside, to himself.*] Oh, damn; I'll bet
I've been drinking again. [*To audience.*] Now you listen! Dammit,
this is important!

    JUDY *turns him around and they move toward the door.*

TIM [*over his shoulder to the audience*]. Now you watch this. Here.

FICK. Terry, you got a cigarette, huh?

AL [*to* TIG]. She's gonna take him!

TERRY [*to* FICK]. Come on, get lost.

KAY [*to* JUDY]. What'd you have?

JUDY. I'll be back!

    JUDY *and* TIM *exit as* DARLENE *enters.*

TERRY. She can sleep in the damn hall for all I care!

RUST [to TERRY]. I don't get it.

AL. It happens every time. Did you see that?

BOB [looks up as DARLENE enters the café]. Well, dig that.

DARLENE *sits at counter*, JOHN *comes to wait on her*.

AL. You get hurt, see? Every time. And then finally you learn not to pay any attention to anything.

TIG. Yeah, I know. Well, don't let it bother you.

BOB [to DARLENE]. Can I buy you a cup coffee? Can I just buy you maybe? Look, I got thirty cents somewhere.

AL. And then you just don't let anything bother you at all.

DARLENE [to JOHN]. Coffee, please.

AL. And you still get hurt.

JOHN [to DARLENE]. Right.

KAY [yelling to JOHN from back]. Draw one!

BOB. You belong here? You new?

KAY [yelling to JOHN]. Two!

TIG [interested in DARLENE now]. She's not the talkative type.

DARLENE [quietly slips off the stool. To JOHN]. Never mind.

She turns to go but there is a crowd at the door. BOB *stands in front of her.*

TIG. Well, don't run off, sweetheart.

FICK [from the back]. It's cold—it gets cold.

DARLENE. Come on.

BOB. I'm sorry if I'm in your way, but I can't move. Look.

DARLENE. Come on, I'm leaving.

TERRY. She can sleep in the alley for all I care!

TIG. Oh, am I in your way?

DARLENE. Oh, screw it. Go away. [*Turns to the counter and sits again.*]

JOHN [to DARLENE]. You order coffee?

TIG. You're new. You know anyone around here?

BOB. Well, be a little sociable anyway. [FRANNY *in exiting bumps against* BOB, BOB *against* DARLENE.] Hey, I'm sorry. [*Turns around, to* FRANNY.] Watch where you're going!

FRANNY. Oh, suck it; if you were sober maybe you could stand up.
                                                            Exits.]

TIG. What are you, mad at the world?

RUST. And she better *stay* gone.

Bob [*to* Tig]. Screw it, forget her. Let's go.

        Dopey *enters café, takes a seat.*

John. Come on, Dopey, you're going to fall asleep.

Tig. Don't bother to speak. [*Goes to the back of café.*]

Bob. Screw it.

Dopey. What do you mean, I'm awake. Look! I want a cup of coffee.

John. I know, but I'll give it to you and you'll be asleep on the damn table. You do it every time, Dopey.

        John *turns to get him coffee.*

Kay [*to* Bob *who has stopped in the doorway*]. Come on, you're holdin' the door open!

Terry [*much louder*]. I don't give a good goddamn if she sleeps with Margaret Truman!   Bob *exits.*]

Dopey [*to prove he's awake*]. Kay? Could you hand me the cream, please?

At the back of the café Terry *falls against a booth. Much commotion. She has spilled coffee on* Bonnie. *They sit her down again.*

Rust, Bonnie, Terry [*variously*].

        Come on.

        God, look at that all over me!

        Where the hell.

        For Christ's sake, where the hell are you going?

        Watch it, fellow.

        Sit down, take it easy.

        All over me. Goddamn.

        Do you have a rag?

        Miss? Now just take it easy.

        Why don't you sober up?

Lights dim for only a second, during the above exchange, with a spot on Darlene.

Al [*to* John]. They every one of them steal. They all steal, you know?

Tig [*to* Ernesto]. Spices and things, you know.

        Ann *re-enters.*

John. Yeah. Well.

        Darlene *and* Joe *exchange several glances.*

Al. Every girl you see; they all steal. You take them up to your room

and they'll steal something every time. You fall asleep and they'll
sneak out and steal something.

TERRY [*over, from the back*]. I'm sorry. I'm sorry. I am.

DOPEY *is falling asleep on the table.*

AL. And then they tell you they left the door open.

JOHN. I know. No, I don't, but I know.

AL. They all steal.

Momentary lull. The quartette begins a soft blues from the back.

JOHN. When it gets quiet in here you almost think something's
gonna happen.

KAY. Quiet all of a sudden, ain't it?

ANN [*to* JOHN]. You want somebody should scream or something?

JOHN. Oh, go back out on the street!

ANN. It's dirty out there. I think I'm going to write to the Depart-
ment of Sanitation. I made sixty tonight.

JOHN. Sixty scores or sixty bills?

ANN. Four scores—ha!—and thirty-eight cents. I always end up with
odd change; never can figure out where the hell it came from.

JOHN. You're so rich, so buy me a drink, teacher.

ANN. Sammy would slug me, I spend his money on you.

TERRY. She can just kiss it.

JOHN. Why do you keep him anyway?

ANN. God, you'd better go back to school.

RUST. Miss, could we have another coffee? Two more.

DARLENE *moves her cup now to the seat by* JOE. *Takes the seat next
to him.*

DARLENE. Do you mind?

JOE. How should I mind?

DARLENE. Well, look, if you're thinking or waiting for someone . . .

JOE. No, I'm not waiting for someone.

DARLENE. I saw you looking at the clock.

JOE. I'm waiting for ten o'clock. [*He drinks. She takes a cigarette
out, he lights hers and his own.*]

DARLENE. Thanks.

TIG [*to* ERNESTO]. You know in Egypt they had salves and things
that could cure anything.

DARLENE. That's better than those other two creeps were acting.
Did you see them?

JOE. They're just high. They're okay usually.

TIG. Cancer even! It says so.

ERNESTO. Show me where, you can't.

TIG. It does.

DARLENE. Why are you waiting for ten o'clock?

TIG. Hey, John; you ever read the Bible?

JOE. I'm meeting someone.

JOHN. What?

TIG. The Bible, stupid.

JOE. Like a business deal. A transaction.

JOHN. Sure. When I was about twelve.

ERNESTO. Yeah?

JOHN. I didn't understand it.

TIG. Hell, you wouldn't anyway. You know they had embalming fluid back then?

ANN. What'd they do, drink it?

ERNESTO. Show me where.

TIG. Go away.

DARLENE. What were they high on?

JOE. Huh? How should I know?

ERNESTO *pays check and exits to corner.*

DARLENE. On dope, or just drinking?

JOE. You don't get high on ginger. Bombinos, deedees; you don't scream it out—you know, you don't yell it out like that.

DARLENE. Do you like that?

JOE. Are you kidding?

DARLENE. Me either—eye-ther.

JOE. Not on your life. Once is enough.

DARLENE. Oh. What was it like?

JOE. Are you kidding? Like getting sick as a bitch. Depends on what you're taking though. New, are you?

DARLENE. Well, have you seen me before?

JOE. No.

DARLENE. Are you sure?

JOE. Yeah.

DARLENE. How do you know?

JOE. I'd know.

DARLENE [*complimented*]. Thanks.

JOE. I remember faces. You see me standing around, you'd think I was just as stupid as the next guy, but I look—and I watch people, you know? And I study them when they don't know. You learn a lot. Where you from?

DARLENE. I'm from Chicago.

TIG [*comes from the booth to* JOHN *at the cash register*]. Could I have change for cigarettes?

DARLENE [*pausing*]. My sister used to come around here, though She's living off somewhere right now.

JOE. Who's your sister?

DARLENE. Oh, you wouldn't know her. It must have been four years ago. She used to write me.

TIG [*hits the machine*]. This damn thing!

DARLENE. Sometimes.

JOE. What'd she do?

DARLENE. Oh, I don't know. [*Affected.*] We used to exchange letters. She'd write and I'd think, God—New York! [*Pause.*] She was . . . like her. [*Nods to* ANN.] Of course, she was very pretty, you know.

JOE. Ann? A hooker. She sold it?

DARLENE. Well, you needn't be high and mighty about it.

JOE. Who is?

DARLENE. She used to make—sometimes a hundred dollars a night . . . twice that sometimes.

JOE. So does Ann, but she loves it. [*Yelling out.*] Don't you, Ann?

ANN. Don't I what?

JOE. Just say yes.

ANN. No. Hell, no; it's a lie if he's saying it. [*Turns away.*]

JOE. She goes for free as much as she charges.

DARLENE. She didn't come here for that, of course. She came here to do something else. I forget what; you know. But you look and you don't get anything and you—resort, you know? To something else.

RUST [*to* TERRY]. I wouldn't worry about it.

JOE. Naw, Ann didn't either. Ann's a schoolteacher. Was going to be; came here to do something like that. When she got here they tell her she can work part-time or something.

TERRY. It doesn't affect me.

JOE. She told 'em to kiss it. She got a raw deal.

DARLENE. Yeah. You know what I'd make as a waitress? Maybe sixty dollars a week. Less maybe. Tips included.

JOE. You been here long?

DARLENE. A month.

JOE. Month? You must have saved up.

DARLENE. Are you kidding? I came here with about seven dollars.

JOE. You get a room around here yet?

DARLENE. I'm across the street, in the Towers. And probably I'll get. . . .

JOE. And one upstairs? Everybody does.

DARLENE. My sister had a room; this same place. I didn't ask you what your ten-o'clock business deal was.

JOE. Yeah, you did.

DARLENE. Well, I didn't care. [*Pause.*] It's a filthy place upstairs. Have you seen it up there? I looked around this afternoon already. I've never seen cockroaches like that. I mean they should get a bravery medal or something. They play games on the floor right in front of you. They don't even run from you.

DOPEY *has awakened. He looks at his coffee and gets up to leave.*

KAY [*to* DOPEY]. Hey, you pay?

DOPEY. I don't have anything.

KAY. Coffee.

DOPEY. I didn't even touch it. I gotta get outside.

He leaves café for corner.

JOE. You know I might be able to help you get a room. Save you some dough, maybe. After the first week or two they'll get on to you and kick you out. They got fellas that hang around to spot girls who take people up. You'll have to get one of the boys around to rent a room in his name and then he'll rent it to you. See? They don't really care, just so long as they look legal. Most of the cats, though, would make you pay through the nose.

DARLENE. Why? I mean why should I get a room from someone else?

JUDY enters and goes to cash register.

JOE. It's just the way you have to do it. All these guys in here—a lot of them—they rent a room out for about eight bucks a night. That's not much when you're making a hundred.

KAY [*to* JUDY]. You owe for a burger and a Coke.

JUDY. I'll get it.

DARLENE. It sounds like a lot to me. Eight dollars a day? A room's only twelve a week. No girl's gonna do that.

JOE. They got nothing better to do with their money. Most of the girls keep a fellow anyway. Give most of their money to some guy.

Then he treats them like shit. Don't ask me. Over half of them.
So they can be seen with someone steady, you know.

JUDY [*regarding* RUST *and* TERRY *in the back booth*]. Well, isn't that
cozy?

DARLENE. I wouldn't believe it. [JOE *shrugs*.] I mean I believe it, but
how can they ever get any money saved up or anything? If they're
giving it away? It's pretty sick, isn't it? Everybody living off everybody like that?

JOE. You won't get away from that, I don't care where you go. You'll
either make a mint of money or go broke. But like I said, most
guys would charge eight bucks. I could probably get you a room
for maybe only four or five.

DARLENE. I don't think so.

JUDY [*to* KAY]. How much do I owe you?

JOE. You'll either go broke or make a pile.

KAY. Ninety-five and that guy's two teas.

DARLENE. I made two hundred dollars one night. That's what I've
been living off of. One guy; man, one night.

JUDY. Just me; he can come back and pay.

JOE. Don't expect it every time.

RUST *comes up to the counter.*

DARLENE. And I didn't have to do anything.

RUST. Give me a glass of water, Kay.

JOE. Much.

KAY. Just hold it a minute!

DARLENE. Nothing. He felt sorry for me or something. He was a
customer—in this café? And the boss fired me. I was right out on
the floor and got fired on the spot. And this guy came over to me
on the floor and said, let's go have a steak or something to eat,
you don't want to work here anyway. Let's go have a steak. He
was my first customer at the café. I walked right off the floor and
we went to his room and he gave me two hundred dollars.

RUST. Could I have a glass of water?

JOE. What, did you roll him?

JUDY [*to* RUST]. First things first, honey!

DARLENE. No! I told you. He gave it to me. He felt sorry for me or
something.

DOPEY *has been standing on the corner, talking to* RAKE. *He turns
to the audience, walks a little away from the others. The action
continues in the café behind him during this speech.*

DOPEY. What he's saying—about renting rooms and all—see—well, there's no reason for it but when a girl—or around here anyway most of the girls have a guy that—kinna looks after them. After all, it's a rough neighborhood; but that's not the only way he looks after them, if you follow my meaning. And the girl sorta keeps him. The guys that are lucky. He lives up in the room—sleeps in the day and the girl uses the room at night. Maybe you think they're being exploited—the girls, I mean, because they don't get ahead. Every dime goes to the john—that's the fellow. And he eventually pulls out—runs off with it—after he's stashed it in a savings account somewhere. But these girls aren't getting so much exploited because they need these guys. No one's forcing them. One leaves, then right after they get over it they're out looking for someone else. Only someone *better*. You know? Like Ann is probably half expecting her john—this guy's name's Sam, or Sammy: she's half expecting him to leave. He's been around seven or eight months; that's about par for Ann. [*Pause.*] Well, it's because they want someone around and because after all balling with old men all the time can get to be a drag—of course not all of their scores are old men. They get just as many good-looking guys; young fellows; high school kids and like that, they pay. Well, maybe you don't like to hear that but they do. So it's not that they get sick of the old men all the time. But these guys that they ball, they aren't—around. You know? They aren't *around*. They want probably to know someone probably. See they're—well. And they don't get new things! I mean these girls don't go out and get themselves dresses and jewelry and things. I mean they get things, but not for themselves, see; for the guy who's with them. New clothes and rings and stuff—all kinds of crap and well because it's no kind of a lark crawling in and out of bed all night and in the morning they maybe want someone who won't leave, see. Won't get up and take off. [*Very quick.*] And then they buy these guys things so the guys around can see how they keep their johns in luxury, you know. [*Pause.*] It's natural as anything. They want someone familiar. You know—to know somebody's touch or their manner or like the texture of his skin. Even if the guy's still asleep in the morning. You can picture it. And this usually keeps them from getting much else. That's what he's trying to tell her only she'll know after a while anyway because it's just a natural thing. So she'll find it out anyway but not till she's there herself.

JUDY [to KAY]. Don't forget the little bitch's glass of water?

RUST [to JUDY]. Who're you talking to?

JUDY. She's gotta wash out a bad taste in her mouth.

RUST. You talking to me, you talk to me.

JUDY. You just take it for what it's worth.

RUST. You got something to say, say it.

FICK. You got a light, Ann?

JUDY. Go on back to the peach in the corner.

JOHN [to RUST]. Sit back down, I'll bring it to you.

RUST [returning to her seat]. Tell her to shut her filthy mouth.

JUDY. You want to know what a filthy mouth is?

JOHN. Come on. . . .

JUDY. I'll rub your face in the sewer you try to . . .

JOHN. Come on, sit down or get out now.

JUDY [sitting immediately]. Give me a coffee!

RUST *sits down at the booth.* DOPEY *walks away from the audience and then comes back, a new thought. A bit irritated.*

DOPEY. You know, though, what—I was thinking what she said; before that, about the cockroaches and all upstairs and she's right, it's a crawling bughouse up there; what really gripes me, she mentioned all the roaches playing like games on the floor up there. A roach's *attitude* just gripes the hell out of me. But what burns me, I've been reading up, not recently, but I saw it somewhere where not only was the roach—that same, exact, goddamn roach that we know—not only were they around about two million years before man, you know, before we came along: Anthropologists or whatever, geologists over in Egypt or somewhere, looking for the first city, they dug down through a city, and straight on down through another, you know, they're piled up like a sandwich or in layers like a seven-layer cake. And they cut down, down through one century to the one before it and the one before that, and every one they found more goddamned cockroaches than anything, and they got before man ever existed and like in the basement of the whole works, there those damn bugs still were, so they've been around, like I said for about a million years before we came along. But not only that! They've made tests, and they found out that a roach can stand—if there was going to be a big atom explosion, they can stand something like *fourteen times* as much radio-whatever-it-is, you-know-activity as we can. So after every man, woman, and child is wiped out and gone, like you imagine, those same goddamn cockroaches will be still crawling around happy as you please over the ruins of everything. Now the picture of that really gripes my ass.

He wanders into the café.

JOE [*reaches into his pocket*]. Did you ever see one of these?

DARLENE. What? What is it, an hourglass?

JOE. Yeah, that lasts about three hours. That's a bombino. That's what Bob had. You asked how he got high.

DARLENE. I don't want it!

JOE. I'm not about to give it to you. It's worth money.

DOPEY. Coffee.

DARLENE. How's it work?

JOHN. Aw, come on, Dopey. You'll just go asleep.

JOE. It works wonders. See?

DOPEY. Whatta you mean?

JOHN ignores him this time.

JOE. That's one jolt in each side. And you break it open, see, and take a tube, a needle and a——

DARLENE. A needle? Oh, God. I thought that's what——[JOE *makes a motion injecting it into his arm.*] That's terrible! That just makes my knees weak.

JOE. I better not let anyone see me doing that; they'll think I'm really taking it. [DARLENE *laughs.*] That's the easy way. I just got one of these. Mostly it's heroin, and that and some of the others you heat up in a spoon with a match.

DARLENE. I don't want to hear it.

JOE. It's a lotta trouble.

DARLENE. And they pay for it?

JOE. Sure. They love it. You gotta sorta coax them along; play with them. They have to get it and they expect it to be tough to get.

BONNIE [*at counter*]. That's highway robbery.

DARLENE. They have to have it. That sounds awful.

JOHN [*to* BONNIE]. Everybody makes a living.

JOE. That's the idea. It doesn't happen overnight or anything.

BONNIE. I'm not complaining.

XAVIER enters.

DARLENE. How much does it cost you?

JUDY [*to* BONNIE]. You get sick of it back there?

JOE. Usually about four. I can make maybe thirty bucks on a carton. Sometimes more. The goofballs are worth about twice as much profit. But they're the devil. They're wild. You never know what the hell they're going to do to someone.

JUDY. What are they saying?

XAVIER. Hey, Joe!

BONNIE. I'm not in it; whatever you're thinking.

JOE. Hi, there, buddy.

JUDY. Well then, just stay out of it then.

XAVIER. You goin' down to Forty-second later?

JOE. Naw, not tonight. I thought I'd turn in.

XAVIER. Nothing's doing down there anyway.

JOE. Stick around here. Where you been the last two days, man?

XAVIER. Around. Sleeping around.

JOE. You still talking about going off? Your old man going to send you some dough?

XAVIER. I don't know. I don't think so, though. I think maybe I'd like to go to Paris, it's better there. People come back from there they say it's wonderful. Beautiful girls.

JOE. So what's wrong with the girls here?

XAVIER [laughing]. Maybe they all know me.

JOE. Maybe. Your friends think Paris is great, huh?

XAVIER. If I go and it's wonderful as that, I'd stay. [BABE coughs. Looks up dreamily and around. Sinks back down. XAVIER looks around to her and back.] Maybe girls here aren't so beautiful. [Laughs.]

JOE. Oh, don't look at Babe. Nobody's like her, man.

DARLENE. What's wrong with her?

XAVIER. She's very bad off.

DARLENE. I've been looking at her.

JOE. You're telling me she's bad off.

XAVIER. She's—you know—that's no good. She can't go a few hours, I bet. She has to have another. She's on her way right out of it. When they get that bad. On her way off.

DARLENE. She's on her way off that stool, anyway.

XAVIER. No, no. A junkie never falls off a stool. They lean out and lean out and they get just to the point and they're way out and their seat is way over there and they start slipping off the stool, and they start shifting back, moving back the other way. A drunk will go right off—*pow*—like that—one jerk and he's on the floor. But a junkie never falls off. You see if I'm wrong.

DARLENE. I didn't know that.

XAVIER. You see if I'm wrong. Look, I'll see you.

JOE. No, come on; stick around.

XAVIER. I'll be back in a few minutes.   *Exits.*]

JOE. He runs around all the time. He says he'll see you soon and you don't meet him for a month. He's a nice guy. *Xavier.* [*He gives it a Spanish pronunciation.*]

DARLENE. What?

JOE. They call him *Xavier.* He's Colombian. His old man owns a bunch of hardware stores down there. He's up here though—and the old man won't give him a cent.

DARLENE. I think he'd be better off back there, then. Is he working?

JOE. Huh? I don't know what he does. He's going to Paris or somewhere next summer.

DARLENE. Huh. What was his name?

JOE [*in English*]. Xavier.

DARLENE. No, the other one.

JOE. *Xavier.* The same thing in Spanish. Like Joe and *José,* you know?

DARLENE. Yeah. Oh.

JOE [*holding the bombino out in his closed hand*]. You want this?

DARLENE. Me? No, no. I don't want that.

JOE. Not to take, I thought maybe you'd want it for a gift to remember me.

DARLENE. I don't think so. Thanks. What if I got caught with it or something. Then where would I be?

JOE. It wouldn't be no worse than getting caught taking some guy up to your room. Same thing. Trouble either way you look.

ERNESTO [*from the corner*]. Hey, Joe. Have you seen Bob?

ERNESTO *and* RAKE *enter the café.*

RAKE. Yeah, you seen him?

JOE [*gets up*]. Yeah, he went up to around Eightieth Street.

RAKE. What time?

JOE [*turns*]. What time, Darlene? The fellow in the orange jacket?

DARLENE. Oh, just a few minutes ago.

ANN. I better be going back out into the dirty street.

JOHN. Yeah, make a little dough.

DARLENE. About fifteen minutes or so ago, I'd imagine.

ANN. Dough's ass; I'm tired.

BONNIE. Back trouble, honey? I know what you mean. You seen King?

ANN. You seen Sam?

JOHN [*to* ERNESTO *and* RAKE]. You gonna order?

BONNIE. Not tonight I haven't.

ANN. Neither have I, the bastard.

ERNESTO. Ain't I a steady paying customer?

JOHN. Are you?

ERNESTO. I am when I got the dough. You find me a john, I'll buy something. Okay? [*To* JOE.] A few minutes ago? I'll see you around. How late you gonna be here?

JOE. Ten, eleven. I'm leaving early.

JOHN. Come on, Rake; you guys. You're blocking the door.

ERNESTO. I'll see you around. [*To* DARLENE.] So long.

RAKE. See you.

They drift back to the corner. DOPEY *gets up, tired of waiting for service and wanders out.*

DOPEY. Shit. Try to get served here.

DARLENE. You saw my name on the purse.

JOE. Yeah.

DARLENE. You said it like we'd been introduced and known each other for years.

JUDY [*at far end of counter, as* RUST *leaves the booth again*]. You really cozy back there, are you?

RUST. What?

JOE. A queer named Jerry Joe got pinched last night. He used to pick up some scores around here. You know? And they caught him with a dozen bombinos on him.

JUDY. You cozy back there?

RUST. Whatta you mean?

JUDY. Whatta you mean, whatta I mean? I got eyes.

DARLENE. The pills?

RUST. Well, whatta you see?

JUDY. I got eyes, goddammit. I can see.

JOE. The other. The pills would have been worse.

RUST. Why don't you go back there, you're so worried.

DARLENE. You better watch yourself then.

JUDY. Go back there! I've had about enough of you.

JOE. They didn't pick him up for that. That's what I was saying. You're telling *me* I'm in a dangerous business.

RUST. Nothing's happening you can't see.

JOE. They picked him up because the stupid fairy tried to pick up a cop. That could happen just as easy to you, you don't play it careful.

JUDY. You sawed-of little bitch, you moving in? You moving into our pad?

DARLENE. I guess you take your chances.

RUST. It'd serve you right if I did.

JUDY. I've had about enough of you.

RUST. Go back to your sick friend.

JOE. It turned out good for me. One of his guys—Martin—came to me already. I'll probably get a few more. He had his finger in everything, Jerry Joe.

JUDY. Get your hot little ass out of here, now.

JOE. Push a little; sell a little. Man, I bet he looked funny when that cop flashed his badge. Serves him right for being so stupid.

TERRY [*standing up, very drunk*]. Just can it now, Judy. Nothing's happening.

FICK [*to* JOHN]. Could I have a coffee? I think. And a bowl of soup? It's getting cold out, huh?

RUST. I'm gonna get this bitch out of my hair.

JOHN [*to* RUST *and* JUDY]. Watch it now.

Phone rings. JOHN *goes to it, answers it.*

RUST [*flares up now*]. You're not gonna get nothing.

JUDY. I'm gonna teach you to break everyone up.

RUST. You're gonna get your ass kicked is what you're gonna get!

JUDY. You little bitch, you can just get the——

She slaps RUST, RUST *returns the slap. They scrap a second, break away,* RUST *has a fork from one of the tables.*

RUST. Okay, you jealous cunt, now you mind your own business.

JUDY [*aware of the spectacle, past anger, hurt now*]. Why don't you mind . . . you stay away from Terry.

RUST. Go slapping people around. I'm not interested in her!

JUDY. You stay away, I saw you!

RUST. You been asking for it all night!

JUDY. *We been together eleven months; you stay away!*

RUST. I'm not bothering her.

JUDY. Go on. . . .

RUST [*throws the fork down*]. I'm leaving.

JOHN [*hangs up phone*]. You people sit down or get out.

RUST. I'm leaving, goddammit.

JOHN [*to all three*]. Come on, clear out. We can't have fights in here.

RUST. Just mind your own business!

TERRY [*to* JOHN]. Nothing's happening.

RUST [*storming out*]. She can pay.

TERRY [*calling to* RUST]. Get your coat.

RUST. I don't want it. [*Out to street corner.*]

JOHN. Now keep it down. That's all out of you two or outside.

TERRY. Bring another coffee over.

JUDY [*whimpering*]. I can't help it.

They talk quietly in the booth.

DARLENE. What's wrong with them?

JOE. Huh? What?

DARLENE. Nothing.

Phone rings. JOHN *answers it.*

JOE [*trying to regain* DARLENE'*s attention*]. In a month or so I'll be making—well, really good money. Some guys like me, they got fellas working for them.

DARLENE. Sure. You know how to handle yourself. That's good. You remind me of this guy I knew in Chicago. Cotton. He knew how to handle himself.

RAKE [*on the corner. To* RUST]. Aren't you cold?

RUST. No.

RAKE. You'll catch cold.

JOHN [*at the phone*]. I'll see. I don't know.

RAKE. You're gonna catch pneumonia.

RUST. Just mind your own business, okay?

JOE. Yeah, well, you learn quick enough. I'll be making really good money. You have to be careful, of course.

DARLENE. Well, who doesn't?

JOE. You'll be all right.

RAKE [RUST *has said something to him quietly*]. I can't go in there either.

JOHN [*comes to the side of* JOE]. Telephone. Sounds like one of Chuckles' fellows. Perry, I think.

JOE. Yeah? Tell him I'll be back in an hour or so.

JOHN. Okay. Don't take calls here—I told you before.

JOE. I didn't ask him to call me here. I'm not going to talk to him here. You know that.

JOHN. Okay.

JOE [to JOHN]. Okay. [To DARLENE.] Besides, the fellow I'm tying in with—Chuckles. That was a friend of his. You don't cross him. You don't cross Chuckles.

KAY. Toast me a muffin.

JOHN. Toasted muffin.

JOE. You don't say yes today and say no tomorrow.

DARLENE. Yeah. I gotta go back over to the hotel.

She gets up.

JOE. I thought you were working.

DARLENE. Working?

JOE. You know.

DARLENE. I thought I'd get to bed and kinna look around the neigborhood tomorrow and see if there's anything open.

JOE. Job?

He gets up.

DARLENE. Or something. If anything's open. You have to live.

JOE. Yeah.

DARLENE. Do you want to walk me across the street? I'd like you to.

JOE. What are you, a little old lady or something? Sure I will; protection.

He pays.

DARLENE. I mean if you're not doing anything.

JOE. No, that's okay.

DARLENE. I won't let you miss your ten-o'clock appointment.

JOE. Screw that. Martin would wait all night.   Exit.]

Dim almost out on café interior. Patrons inside walk to the front of the café and stand in a line across stage, back to the audience, forming a "wall." There is a space about four feet wide at the center of the wall, forming a doorway. JOE and DARLENE walk down the wall slowly.

DARLENE. I haven't seen the neighborhood at daytime yet.

JOE. Neither has anybody else.

DARLENE. I'll bet.

KAY [from the café, distantly]. Scramble two with bacon, John.

DARLENE. It's getting cold.

JOE. Yeah.

DARLENE. There was snow last night.

JOE. Was there?

DARLENE. Not much. It didn't stick. Just a little. It's too early for snow.

> *She walks inside the doorway and turns. He is outside.*

JOE. Yeah, you'd think so.

DARLENE. Look, I don't want you to be late for your meeting, if you're meeting someone.

JOE. It isn't important. What do you have in mind?

DARLENE. I don't know. Do you want to come up? You can. I'd like for you to. You know. If you want to.

JOE. Yeah, I'd like that. [RAKE *leaves his place in the wall and comes toward the audience.*] I been thinking about just that for the last hour.

DARLENE. Me too, really.

> *They go through the "door," out of sight behind the "wall" of people.*

JOHN [*from the café*]. You're sure as hell not going to make any money like that!

> *The "wall" moves to close the doorway behind them.*

RAKE [*to the audience*]. You travel around. I mean hustlers travel around, after all they follow the sun, staying where the weather's warm. In New York, north, you know, when it's hot here. And in the winter they begin to drift down toward Miami Beach so it's warm. And out to California. All around. You hear a lot about Miami Beach but you don't hear that it's winter quarters for about half the hustlers in the country. I guess they don't advertise that—but the johns know it. A hustler tries to keep where it's warm. I don't know if it's because of warm weather and all or whether they just try to keep up a good tan, you know? What the hell, it's healthy. But you travel around and you start seeing differences in people. In the way people act from one place to another. Like in New York—the main difference between people in Chicago and New York is in New York everyone carries an umbrella. If it's the least bit cloudy you can depend on it, every goddamn plumber or electrician or construction worker or executive in New York carries an umbrella. It's just the way they think. They don't think about it. But see, Chicago, there it's this symbol or something. See in Chicago you're never going to see a construction worker carrying one of those narrow little rolled-up rapier kind of umbrellas. Or any other kind. It's unmasculine, see.

They won't have it. In New York, sure; but in Chicago, not on your life. Fairies and old women, some, not many, carry umbrellas when it's really cloudy. But everyone else stays clear of that sort of thing. [*Pause.*] Consequently they get rained on a lot in Chicago.

The "wall" disperses. People move off and back to the café, in every direction. There has been a bed set up behind the wall. JOE *is in undershorts. He sits on the edge of the bed, then lies back, propped up on his elbow.* DARLENE *has just slipped on a half-slip and bra. She stands over the bed for a moment. Then moves away a bit. The scene should be dimly lit.* RAKE *walks off.*

DARLENE [*a little breathless*]. Oh, Lord. I'm all over sweat—perspiration. So are you. Look at you. Do you want a cigarette? How about that?

Joe remains uninterested in her throughout this scene; quite remote.

JOE. Sure.

DARLENE. Jesus. [*She hands him a package of cigarettes and matches.*] Here you are, baby. [*Walking away.*] Let me get a towel. I feel like I'd gone for a swim. I'm wet and all, but I mean, my legs and arms weigh a ton; I just feel like I'd been swimming for hours. I'll get a towel or something, how's that? [JOE *lights a cigarette.*] I thought I'd swipe this towel when I move, when I get an apartment of my own. It's got the name of the hotel across it. I thought that'd be funny; hanging in a regular bathroom. [*She dries her neck and arms on the towel.*] Oh, that's more like it. Here, let me. You're perspiring like a maniac.

JOE. Throw it over.

DARLENE. Here. [*She rubs his belly.*]

JOE. Come on!

DARLENE. It's not going to hurt you.

She starts to dry his chest and face, JOE *pulls back.*

JOE. Come on, Darlene. For Chris' sake! [*Pushing her gently away.*] For Chris' sake! [*He takes the towel.*]

DARLENE. What? You take it then. Where did you put the cigarettes?

JOE. Over here.

DARLENE [*artificially gay, goes to them*]. Oh, swell. Lord. What time are you supposed to see that guy?

JOE. What guy?

DARLENE. I don't know. The guy that you're supposed to see. I don't know his name.

JOE. Oh, for Chris' sake, I told you, Martin hangs around that corner all night long. If I miss him at ten he's around at eleven. It isn't important. He'll be there. He's a junkie.

DARLENE. Looks to me like you all hang around there all night.

JOE. Well it's an important place around here.

DARLENE. You made it sound so mysterious.

JOE. I don't have to answer to him. That's for damn sure. [He puts his shirt and pants on, bragging.] Look, you want to know something? You want to know something? I knew what I was doing. I keep a sharp lookout for myself, you don't have to worry about that. I watch people and size them up. And this guy Chuckles you heard me mention?

DARLENE. Yeah?

JOE. The guy who had someone call me back at the café. Now, this guy is probably the most important pusher—he doesn't push himself, but he supplies—and you don't screw around with him. I got in touch with Chuckles a while back and told him I wanted to get cut in. Make some dough around the neighborhood. Hell, he'd been watching me for weeks. Months! And we made this deal. He gave—not give!—Chuckles never gave anyone the time of day. But he loaned—on credit—you know? He loaned me about a hundred dollars' worth of stuff. . . .

DARLENE. What kind of . . .

JOE. Dope. Heroin. I told you. . . .

DARLENE. What do you do with it? You sell it to that guy?

JOE. On credit. See, I sell it now and make twice or more profit. All I give him is his hundred. But see there's this—it's not this once only. If you're in with this guy like I wanted to be, you're in for a while. And chances are, like almost everyone you'll get picked up. A guy just starting runs all the risks. You can be about so clever. But once I sell that stuff—see, I'm in up to my throat. Hell, I'm in already. You don't butt out on Chuckles. You don't just carry it around.

DARLENE. You don't sound very pleased about it.

JOE. He loaned it to me for twenty-four hours, you know? And they been up a long time now. Day before yesterday. I just can't think straight on it. You don't cross him, though.

DARLENE. I guess not, but if you think it's too dangerous. . . .

JOE. The sentence for pushing *H* is about thirty years! Hell, I'm the same as in with Chuckles already.

DARLENE. I thought you just was. But if you don't want to be, you could talk with. . . .

JOE [*getting up*]. Christ!

DARLENE. No, really. I've always felt if people just talked about their problems they can always work something out. . . .

JOE. Yeah, sure. What time is it?

DARLENE. I don't know. Let's see.

JOE. You want to call down and ask the desk?

DARLENE. No. I have a wrist watch, I'm not that poor.

JOE. What time is it?

DARLENE. Well, I'm trying to read it, it's small! It's one-thirty.

JOE. Christ! Oh, Christ!

The people who have left the stage begin to drift in in the background, occasionally crossing in front.

FICK. Hey, hey, Tig?

TIG. Sure, don't even ask. Any time. Christ. [*Takes a cigarette and gives it to* FICK.]

DARLENE. Why, do you have to go somewhere?

FICK [*badly wetting and destroying the end of the cigarette*]. God, look at me slobber all over it. I'm a mess. Jesus.

JOE. Jesus. [*He puts on his jacket.*]

DARLENE. Do you have to go somewhere?

JOE. Yeah. I'll see you tomorrow or if you come back tonight.

FICK. I'm such a damn slob. Look at that. I'll get it though. [*Wanders back into café.*]

JOE *goes into the café.* DARLENE *exits. The bed is removed. Lights up on café; very late at night.* ANN *is considerably more disheveled. As lights go up the first rock'n'roll song blasts out of the juke box.* JOHN *immediately reaches under the counter and turns it down.*

TIG. Hey, that's my song.

JOHN [*over, to* JOE *as he enters*]. Martin was looking for you, Joe.

JOE. Let him look. When?

JOHN. God, I don't know; hours ago. Chuckles called you on the phone.

JOE. *He did?* [*Shrugs.*] Coffee. What did you tell him?

JOHN. I told him you left early.

JOE [*with a swagger*]. What does he want with me?

JOHN [*knowingly*]. Yeah, I wonder, huh.

JOE. How'd you get it so quiet in here?

JOHN. Wait ten minutes. It'll be a madhouse. We had a dishwasher walk out.

JOE. I never knew you had one.

ANN [*entering*]. Coffee, okay, John?

JOHN. Coffee for teacher.

ANN. Oh, can it. Did you see that john? That last one?

JOHN. See who?

ANN. That fellow I took up.

JOHN. No.

JOE. Naw.

ANN. God, was he sick.

JOHN. You get all kinds, huh?

ANN. All kinds and varieties.

JOHN. How much was he worth?

ANN. Fifteen. What the hell. You seen Sam? He's not been around?

JOHN. Your boy friend? No.

ANN. God, was he sick. Hey this guy last night—you should have seen him. He had a roll of bills, I've never seen anything like it. He owns some gas stations around—three or four and he'd just made the rounds and collected from them. He must have had six or eight hundred. And I'm feeding him booze and walking the floor trying to figure some way of getting it and he's getting ready to leave. And I keep talking about everything I can think of. Pulling him back. God, I'll bet he thought he'd got hold of an eager demented whore for sure. I nearly went nuts. Kept him in the room for an hour trying to think of some way to get it.

FICK [*to* TIG *in the back booth*]. You notice how cold it's getting?

JOHN. Can't you stick to an honest living?

FICK. Bet it snows. Me with no goddamned overcoat.

ANN. Ha. He must have had six hundred. [*Pause.*]

FICK. Goddamn.

ANN. What the hell, who needs it? [*To* JOE.] What are you so quiet about anyway?

JOE. Can't I be quiet?

ANN. Sit over there like the bird that caught the cat.

JOE. Can't I be quiet?

ANN. No. Oh, hell. [*Gets up.*]

At the back a STRANGER, *who has entered, gets up to pay his check.*

ANN. Oh, hell. Hell, hell, hell, hell, hell. [*Wanders out.*]

STRANGER [*to* JOE]. You Joe Conroy?

JOE. Who are you?

STRANGER. Are you Conroy?

JOE. What are you? Some kind of cop or something?

STRANGER. You pretty big around here?

JOE. Who, me?

STRANGER. You must be thinking you're pretty hot stuff around here.

JOE. Hey, John, could I have cream with this, huh?

STRANGER. You don't screw around with Chuckles; you don't cross Chuckles, Conroy. You ought to know that.

JOE. What's that?

STRANGER. You're a little late, and we understand. But business is business. So we'll have to have interest on the little loan.

JOE. Like what?

STRANGER. Like a hundred a day—every day you're late. Man, that's sad news. You're due to lose money at that rate, you know?

[*Exits.*]

JOE. I'm not crossing nobody. Beginning when? Hey. [*Pause for a second.*] Hey, John. You know that guy?

JOHN [*from the far end of the counter, looks up*]. No. Never saw him, don't think.

JOE. I think he's some kind of cop.

BOB [*entering with* TIM]. Yeah, yeah, yeah; whatta you think, whatta you think? Hey, John, we'll take a booth—coffee and we'll leave, okay?

JOHN. Fifty cents a person minimum.

BOB. Come on. Whatta you thinking about?

TIG. Hey, buddy.

BOB. Whatta you thinking?

JOHN. Fifty cents.

TIM. Since when?

JOHN. Since year one. Look, do I own the place or do I work here? I work here.

BOB [*to* TIG]. Spare me a dollar till tomorrow morning, okay? I gotta pay someone before he——

TIG. I got no dollar.

Lights begin to fade on the scene.

DOPEY [*to* RAKE *and* ERNESTO *on the corner*]. It's here, right? This is it.

RAKE. No, God. Not yet.

JOHN. Sit somewhere.

BOB. Come on, tomorrow morning.

DOPEY. It is, go on, man; get it there.

RAKE [*pushing him back*]. Come on.

FICK. Damn, is it getting cold, man? Do you know what happened, Tig? To me? You know why I'm so mussed up? Did I tell you?

BOB. Just a minute. We'll take a booth, okay?

FICK. I told you, huh.

JOHN. Fifty cents a person.

BOB. Oh, for Chris' sake.

FICK. Do I, Tig? Do I?

TIG. Do you what, Fick? I don't know what you're talking about.

RAKE [*under his breath to* ERNESTO *and* DOPEY]. Okay, this is it.

The lights are very dim on café. ERNESTO, RAKE, *and* DOPEY *come forward (downstage center) to audience.*

ERNESTO. We got this song here; we do this song.

DOPEY. Read it.

RAKE. I'll say it first, so you know the words or you couldn't make it out.

DOPEY. It's a round.

RAKE. It's a round and you can't understand the words if you don't know them.

DOPEY. And the name is—see . . .

ERNESTO. It's about us.

RAKE. Yeah. The name is—see it's us; this is our song about us.

DOPEY. We stand around on the corner all night, see, and don't do nothing.

RAKE. You know, with our hands in our pockets like. Come on, Bob; you're in this—Tim, come on.

TIM *and* BOB *come to the group.*

BOB. What's up?

RAKE [*to* BOB]. Wake up!

ERNESTO [*over*]. And the name is "Men on the Corner." Fellows on the corner, like that.

RAKE [*ready to read the words from a piece of paper that he has taken from his pocket*]. Okay.

ERNESTO [*to audience*]. I'm not in it. [*Goes into the café.*]
RAKE. It's this round. This is just the words:

> They laugh and jab
> cavort and jump
> and joke and gab
> and grind and bump.

DOPEY [*quickly*]. See? It's us.
RAKE.

> They flip a knife
> and toss a coin
> and spend their life
> and scratch their groin.
>
> They pantomime
> a standing screw
> and pass the time
> with nought to do.
>
> They swing, they sway
> this cheerful crew,
> with nought to say
> and nought to do.

DOPEY *begins the round as soon as* RAKE *is finished, followed by*
TIM *and* BOB *and* RAKE *in that order. The melody is shockingly
gentle; rocking; easy; soft; lilting.*

They laugh and jab ca-vort and jump and joke and gab and grind and bump. They

flip a knife and toss a coin and spend their life and scratch their groin. They

pan-to-mime a stand-ing screw and pass the time with nought to do. They

swing, they sway this cheer-ful crew with nought to say and nought to do.

In the background with a minimum of extraneous movement the people in the café silently lift every stick of furniture, the "set," about three feet off the ground and turn the set—as a turntable would—walk the set in a slow circle until it is facing the opposite direction as at the beginning. They set the furniture down in place and sit. The round ends.

DOPEY [*as the last line of the round is sung*]. See, the words of this one make some sense anyway. If you read the other one—the 'rock'n'roll at the beginning of the show—it would sound like this: y-ooo, y-ooo, yackie-yackie do, y-ooo, y-ooo, yackie, yackie. . . .

ERNESTO [*to* DOPEY]. Come on.

DOPEY. "What would I do yackie, yackie do, y-ooo, y-ooo. . . .

ERNESTO. Let's go.

DOPEY. Isn't that a bitch?

RAKE. Come on. Bob, you and Tim go on back. [TIM *and* BOB *enter café as* DOPEY *and* RAKE *go back to the street corner. To the audience.*] We'll see you.

Lights up in the café.

FICK. You didn't see it, Tig; I tell you they had me pinned, man. Down in this hall-thing. Four or five big black cats, they must have been huge. . . .

DARLENE [*entering the café*]. Hi, Joe.

JOE. Hi.

DARLENE. Couldn't sleep. I thought you might be here.

JOE. Sure.

All of FICK's *dialogue in this scene is over* DARLENE *and* JOE's *scene, as a background. Very soft at first here.* FICK *is in the back of the café. To* TIG *who is not listening.* FICK's *dialogue is continuous.*

FICK. I mean, big, strong fellows; fighters. They pushed me into this doorway. Right into the door, and down this hall and back into this dark place there in the hall there.

DARLENE. What's wrong?

JOE. Whatta you mean?

DARLENE. You look like something was wrong is all.

JOE. Do I?

DARLENE. What's wrong? You can tell me.

JOE. Nothing, goddammit. Come on—you come in here and in three seconds flat you start telling me I'm crazy or something.

DARLENE. I didn't say anything like that.

JOE. Hell you didn't.

FICK. See, they thought I had a bottle on me, and I said I don't drink, and they didn't know I was high, you know. And they're standing over me and they feel around and see I don't have any money on me and I said, shit, man, you think I walk around with money? I mean, look at me now, do I look like I carry money around with me? I don't have any money on me.

DARLENE. I just asked. Hell! Look at you!

JOE. Don't look at me then.

DARLENE. What's bugging you anyway?

JOE. Nothing. Dammit. Darlene. [Nicer.] What the hell am I going to do with you anyway?

DARLENE [nicer]. I don't know. I swear I don't. You let me know when you come up with something, though, you hear?

JOE. Yeah. I'll think of something. [Pause in their conversation.]

FICK. I get four dollars, I shoot it, man it's all I can afford. About twenty dollars a day, man, most days I don't even know where it came from, cause I'm high, man, and I don't remember, I can't think. And they start roughing me up and I said, man, you got the wrong boy. Why don't you rough up someone your own size?

JOE. You want a cup of coffee?

DARLENE. Sure. Why not. John? I won't sleep now, anyway. [Pause.] Did you get back in time to see that Martin?

JOE. Oh, Christ. What the hell difference does it make? I told you I don't owe him nothing.

DARLENE. I didn't know. I take it from that you didn't get back in time.

JOE. What business is it of yours, anyway?

DARLENE. Well, I just wondered. For Christ's sake. If you can't even be civil.

FICK. I mean even if I was a big cat, see, I'm small, but even if I was a big cat I wouldn't go roughing up people like that. They fairly gave me hell, and beat the tar out of me. I just balled up in the hall there and didn't move, I mean, if I get up they're going to get at my face and all, and I just balled up and had to take it.

JOE. Well, if you have to nose into everybody's business.

DARLENE. I don't give a good goddamn if you saw him or not. Or Chuckles even.

JOE. Then why the hell did you bother to ask?

DARLENE. Forget it. Christ. Excuse me for living.

JOE. Just keep your nose in your own business. You have business of your own to worry about. Darlene, for Christ's sake.

FICK. 'Cause I couldn't get even one good punch in at them. I couldn't get one good punch at them. I mean, look at me, I'm weak as a kitten. What would you expect, I started shooting *H* when I was about thirteen. And hell, that's a long time ago now; I mean I wasn't a tough kid or nothing like that, but I could protect myself, you know, I could spar around, but Christ I can't even see anything half the time, I can't follow things around you know and they're kicking me around the hallway there.

TIG starts to get up, sits back down.

DARLENE. Pardon me for living.

JOE. Go get laid. You can't mind your own business. You come in here and . . .

DARLENE. Jesus. Just forget it.

JOE. Okay. It's forgotten. [*Pause.*]

FICK. No, don't go away now, listen to this, just listen to me now. See these guys were kicking me around and I can't do nothing. But what I'm saying, if I could get a couple of big guys, you know, a few big guys, you know, a few big guys and go up there, go back there.

DARLENE. Christ! [*Pause.*]

JOE. You want coffee?

DARLENE. I don't know.

JOE. Suit yourself.

DARLENE. Yeah. Okay John?

JOHN. Got it.

JOE. Christ.

DARLENE. Are you in trouble? Be serious now.

JOE. Yes. Dammit, there. You feel better now?

FICK. I couldn't do nothing myself, I mean, I just laid there, man. But if I could just get a couple of big guys, a couple of fighters and go back there. No, don't run off, I'm not talking about you, but you're big fellows, you could look big. See I know these mothers; I seen them around here all the time. And they know I don't have any bread, they know that.

TIG moves to a different seat. FICK continues as if TIG were still there.

DARLENE. Is it serious?

FICK. But with a couple of fellows, fighters, they'd run like hell, they wouldn't start nothing, you'd see.

JOE. Yes.

FICK. They'd run like a couple of scared mothers. I mean we wouldn't have to do nothing or nothing, they'd just turn tail and get the hell out of there.

DARLENE. Are you going to work for him?

JOE. I don't have much of a choice. One of his friends—one that I'd never seen before—paid me a visit here to inform me I'd owe Chuckles a hundred bucks a day interest till I paid him off. Now are you happy?

FICK. See, they'd think I had friends, see, and they'd know not to fuck with me any more, as soon as they saw I had a couple of friends they'd not mess around with me, you know what I mean?

DARLENE. You can't get money like that, can you? Can you? What are you going to do, Joe?

JOE. I don't know yet! I don't know. What, yet. I gotta think.

They sit quietly, looking up out toward the street.

FICK. I mean, I was just walking down the street and they came up on me like they was important, and they start pushing me around, you know. And they pushed me into this alley, not an alley, but this hallway and back down the end of that to this dark place at the end of the hallway and they start punching at me, and I just fell into this ball on the floor so they couldn't hurt me or nothing. But if I came down there with a couple of fighters, a couple of guys, like my friends, it wouldn't have to be you or anything, but just a couple or three guys, big guys, like walking down the street, you know. Just so they could see I got these buddies here. See I'm on *H*, I mean, I'm flying and I gotta talk man, but I'm serious now; just a few guys and they'd leave me be, maybe, because they'd think I had these buddies that looked after me, you know; cause I—you know—they kicked me up, if I wasn't on *H*, man, they'd be pains all through me—you know—walking down the street by myself—I start looking around and wondering who's out there gonna mess me up, you know. I get scared as hell, man, walking down around here, I mean, I can't protect myself or nothing, man. You know what I mean? You know what I mean? You know what I mean? You know? I mean if I had these couple

—of big buddies—fighters—you—you know—if I had a couple of guys—like—big guys—that—you know, there's like nothing—I could—like, if you walked around with these buddies, I mean you could do, man—you could do anything. . . .

Long pondering pause. He looks to everyone one at a time. No one moves. He turns and looks at BABE. *She raises her head as if to speak and very slowly looks back down to the counter.*

DOPEY [*on the corner. Turns to audience. Clearly*]. We'll call an intermission here.

Curtain.

DARLENE. Isn't that terrible, I forgot his last name. I just blanked out.

ANN. Conroy.

DARLENE. Yes, I know. I remember it now.

ANN. Sure. I've seen you with Joe, I know now.

DARLENE. I'm Darlene.

ANN. Fine.

DARLENE. Joe said you came to New York to be a teacher.

ANN. Oh, God.

DARLENE. Didn't you?

ANN. Who remembers?

DARLENE. And you're from Nebraska. I'm from Chicago, so that's not far off.

ANN. Minnesota.

DARLENE [*puzzled for a moment—smiles*]. Illinois.

ANN. I'm from Minnesota. You're from Chicago.

DARLENE. Oh. Minnesota. I said something else, didn't I? [*Pause.*] I been here about a month, I guess. He—Joe—talked about you a lot.

ANN. He must have!

DARLENE. Oh, it was all good! [*Realizes it couldn't have been good. Embarrassed hesitation.*] I saw you this afternoon.

ANN. Me?

DARLENE. I was up early for a change; I had to go down to Port Authority and get some things I'd left there. You were walking down uh—uh—over toward that church; the whichever one—I don't know—there's a market there and a bakeshop.

ANN. I don't know.

DARLENE. Yes, you do. You were with this guy. Probably your boy friend. Real big fellow.

ANN. Boy friend for the next fifteen minutes probably— Oh, no! That was Sam. That *is* my boy friend. If you can call it that. He dragged me out of bed to look at a TV set some bum friend of his mopped from a PR apartment. Ratty old contraption. He couldn't get either one of us focused.

DARLENE [*has been listening too intently, too amused*]. Huh?

ANN. Some clunk friend of his was trying to fence a bum set for twenty-five bucks. I dragged him down to some store and bought a new one.

DARLENE. Really? That's wonderful.

ACT TWO

Early evening. Only FRANK, ANN, JUDY, *and* TERRY *are in t*
ANN is the only person seated at the counter.

DARLENE [*enters the café. She sits a few stools from* ANN].
have a coffee, please?

FRANK [*in a rather good mood*]. Sure, miss.

DARLENE. John isn't on yet, huh? He come on about seven?

FRANK. Yeah.

DARLENE. And I think maybe—what's the little cupcake? A
chocolate all through?

FRANK. White. Chocolate frosting.

DARLENE. Oh. No. Nothing else, I guess. I'm not really hung

She looks toward ANN. DARLENE *drinks a moment and*
great deal of milk into the coffee.

FRANK. Watch that milk—all that's not good for you.

You should have the feeling he's more worried about the
milk.

DARLENE. It isn't?

FRANK. It'll make you fat.

He walks to the far end of the counter.

DARLENE. Oh, that's one thing I don't worry much about. [*S*
toward ANN *who is drinking coffee and smoking a cigare*
ing out the window in a half-dream.] Isn't your nan
[*Pause. No reaction.* ANN *probably hasn't heard her.*]
thought, if you're busy or. . . .

ANN [*turns to her. Does not recognize her at first*]. Yes?

DARLENE. I don't know many people around the neighborl
I've seen you around. A friend of mine knows you real
knows you, I think.

FRANK *sits at one of the booths, reading a paper.*

ANN. Joe? Conroy? Chuckles' fellow? Or is he?

DARLENE. I don't—short—but not too short. Real cute—s
hair. I don't think he's Chuckles' fellow, but he know
believe.

ANN. Conroy. God yes, I know Joe.

47

ANN. He didn't like it, of course. There wasn't anything that needed to be done on it. Tinkered with. He didn't want to watch it unless he could conquer it first. His room is one solid mass of parts and tubes and coils and wires and various masculine symbols like that. Of course, *he* is one solid mass of—but that's another conversation altogether. You're from Chicago. I went to Chicago when I was about four, I think.

DARLENE. Really? Yeah, I grew up there. It's not like New York at all.

ANN. Yeah.

DARLENE. I know what you mean about radio parts and nuts and bolts and everything. That's funny, the way you put it. [*Pause.*] Oh, I like New York all right, I guess. It's like a whole different place, you know.

ANN. I imagine.

DARLENE. I mean back home is like a small town compared to here.

ANN. For me, too.

MARTIN *enters café.*

DARLENE. You're from Minnesota?

ANN. Ashville, Minnesota.

MARTIN. Pardon me. Ann. Right?

ANN. Yes?

MARTIN [*mumbles*]. I thought so; I wondered, there's this guy I've . . .

ANN. Speak up, baby, I can't hear you.

MARTIN. I said, there's this guy, I know he comes around here.

ANN. Who's that?

MARTIN. I don't know, I know I heard he was around here, I've seen him around. Spanish fellow, dark . . .

ANN. I don't think I can help you on that one, there's a *lot* of Spanish guys floating around here. [*She starts to turn away.*]

MARTIN. He's a Colombian guy; dresses very smart.

ANN. Are you talking about Xavier?

DARLENE. That's who I was gonna say, *Xavier.*

MARTIN. Yes, yes, that's him; that's him.

ANN. Sure, everybody knows Xavier.

MARTIN. Have you seen him around today?

ANN. I don't think so.

MARTIN [*overlapping*]. Has he been in here today?

ANN. Not that I know of.

MARTIN. A Colombian guy, very smart dress——

ANN. Yeah, I know who you mean. [*To* DARLENE.] Sorry, you were saying it's——

MARTIN. Do you know where he'd be; or where he lives or anything?

ANN. No, I'm afraid I don't.

DARLENE. He's been around this week, though. With *Xavier* you never know when you're going to see him.

ANN. He runs around a lot.

DARLENE. He says I'll be right back and you won't see him for a month sometimes.

ANN. Sorry. [*Pause.*]

MARTIN. Yeah. [*Pause.*]

DARLENE [*to* ANN]. That guy that you were with, the tall——

MARTIN [*overlapping, conversational level*]. You don't suppose that he'll be in right away?

ANN. I tell you what, you could undoubtedly catch him later on this evening; why don't you come back?

MARTIN. Yeah. I just wanted to see him about something.

ANN. Well, if it's important I could——

MARTIN. No, no. It's not important.

ANN. If I see him do you want me to tell him to stick around?

MARTIN. No. No, that's okay. I'll probably run into him, you know, this evening. Thank you.

ANN. Sure.

FRANK. You want something?

MARTIN. No, no, thanks.

FRANK. Coffee or something. It's getting cold out.

MARTIN. No, I'll be back, no thanks.

DARLENE. What was the fellow's name again?

ANN. Him? I don't know, I've seen him around.

DARLENE. No, the tall guy; you know, that I saw you with?

ANN. Sam?

DARLENE. Yeah. You're not married to him, are you?

ANN. God, no.

DARLENE [*laughs*]. I know what you mean. That's funny. [*Pause.*] Those two that always sit around in here, you know; the dark headed one and she's got a little baby? Are they married? Or do you know?

ANN. I don't know. No one knows. I don't imagine, but they'd probably tell you they were.

DARLENE. It's a cute little baby, really. I don't know if I'd bring him here at all hours of the day and night like that if it was mine, though.

ANN. Well, some people would give anything to look respectable.

DARLENE [*pause*]. I know one thing: I sure feel like you do about marriage. I mean, I just don't know. Like you said. I know this guy I used to go with—when I first got a room of my own, up on Armitage Street? Do you know that part of Chicago?

ANN. No. But then I was only four.

DARLENE. Oh. Well, most of the streets run either east and west or up and down, you know—one or the other. But some of them kinna cut across all the others—Armitage Street does, and some of the other real nice ones. Fullerton Street does.

I don't know if it's important, but Fullerton Street does not. In other words, DARLENE *rather prefers the vivid to the accurate.*

DARLENE. And they're wider, you know, with big trees and all, and there are all of these big old lovely apartment buildings, very well taken care of, with little lawns out front and flower boxes in the windows and all. You know what I mean? And the rents, compared to what they try to sock you with here. The rents are practically nothing—even in this neighborhood. [*Pause.*] My apartment was two flights up, in the front. It was so cute, you'd have loved it. They had it all done over when I moved in. I had three rooms. And let's see—there was just a lovely big living room that looked out onto Armitage Street and a real cute little kitchen and then the bedroom—that looked out onto a garden in the back and on the other side of the garden was Grant Park—or some park, I never did know the name it had. But there were kids that I just loved playing out in this park all the time. And then I had this little bathroom, a private bath. I had—it was funny—I had a collection—you know practically everybody collects something. . . .

ANN. Yeah, I know what you mean.

DARLENE [*laughs*]. No, not like that! I collected towels, if you must know. You know, from all the big hotels—— Of course, I didn't get very many of them myself, but friends of mine, every time they went anywhere always brought me back a big bath towel or hand towel or face towel with some new name across it. I'll swear, I never bought one towel in all the time I lived there! It was funny, too, it looked real great in a regular bathroom like that; these hotel names. Everyone just loved it. My favorite one was—from this—oh, this real elegant hotel—what was it's—I don't even remember the name any more I had so many of them. Anyway, the apartment, in that neighborhood and all, cost me practically nothing compared to what they want for a place not half as good in New York. And I lived there, and this guy I was going with, you know, that asked me to marry him? He lived across the hall. He moved into the apartment next to mine. Really, Ann, you should have seen him. He was slow, everything he did, and quiet; he hardly ever talked at all. You had to just pump him to get him to say the time of day. And he had white hair—nearly white; they used to call him Cotton—he told me—when he was in Alabama. That's where he's from. He was living in the apartment next to mine and we were always together, and there just wasn't any difference between his place and mine. We should have only been paying for one rent. Half of his stuff was in my place and half vice versa. He used to get so pissed off when I'd wash things out and hang them up in his bathroom or in the kitchen and all. You know, over the fire there. But we were always together—and we finally decided to get married—we both did. And all our friends were buying rice and digging out their old shoes. Cotton —he worked in a television factory, RCA, I believe, but I couldn't be sure. That's why I started thinking about him when you said this Sam had electrical parts all over the apartment. Old Cotton had, I'll swear, the funniest temperament I ever saw. If he got mad —[*Almost as though mad.*]—he wouldn't argue or anything like that, he'd just walk around like nothing was wrong only never say one word. Sometimes for two or three days. And that used to get me so mad I couldn't stand it. Have you ever known anyone who did that?

ANN. Yeah, I know what you mean.

DARLENE. Just wouldn't talk at all, I mean. Not say one word for days.

ANN. It sounds familiar enough.

DARLENE. It used to just burn me up. And he knew it did, is what made it so bad. I'd just be so mad I could spit. And I'd say something like: *what's wrong, Cotton?* And just as easy as you please he'd reach over and light a cigarette and look out the window or something. Turn on the radio. I just wish I had the control to be like that because it is the most maddening thing you can pos-

sibly do to someone when they're trying to argue with you. I
could do it for about five minutes, then I'd blow my stack. Oh,
I used to get so damn mad at him. *Agh!* [*Pause.*] Course I make it
sound worse than it was, cause he didn't act like that very often.
Fortunately. But you never knew what was going to provoke him,
I swear. It was just that we saw each other every hour of every
day—you just couldn't get us apart. And when we decided to get
married all our friends were so excited—of course, they'd been
expecting it probably. But we were so crazy you'd never know
what we were going to do. I know he used to set the TV so it
pointed into the mirror, because there wasn't a plug-in by the
bed and we'd lay there in bed and look at the mirror that had the
TV reflected in it. Only everything was backwards. Writing was
backwards. [*She laughs.*] Only, you know, even backwards, it was
a better picture, it was clearer than if you was just looking straight
at it.

ANN. Yeah. So did you?

DARLENE. Get married? Oh, Lord, it was such an or*deal!* We got—
now you have to know Cotton for this to be funny to you—but
when he went for his blood test I nearly died laughing. He's got
these real pale eyes and just no color, you know—a pink color all
over him; absolutely the lightest-skinned person I've ever known
who wasn't sickly or something. They called him an albino; you
know what that is?

ANN. Yes.

DARLENE. It's a kind of horse. And Cotton's eyes were kinda pink
and trying to be blue, so they came out a kind of lavender. You'd
have thought he couldn't be a lighter color and be alive. And
when the doctor stuck the needle in him, oh, Lord, he faded out
like a dollar shirt. I've never seen anyone in my life get that white
in three seconds flat. I don't mean he fainted or anything, but
you should have seen him. He was so damn scared it was really
great of him, because he didn't make a fuss or anything. I said,
honey, do you want to sit down or something? And he just said,
oh, no. Cotton wasn't weak either—he was tough as they make
'em. He was pale and all like I said, but he was strong as an ox
and rough. He was always in some fight, beating the pants off
someone or other. [*Chattier.*] We went to this doctor Lillian—
a girl friend of mine—went to when she thought she was pregnant, but she wasn't, thank God. And I think it was the follow-

ing Saturday, the license office was only open till noon or one
o'clock, I remember. And Cotton was supposed to work, but he
got off; we went up to City Hall for our license. They're building
a new building for City Hall in Chicago, or I think they are.
I *hope* they are! They didn't have any air conditioning or anything—naturally, and of course it was in the middle of summer:
July eleventh. On a Saturday. Anyway, this old building covers
a whole block, right out to the sidewalk and it must be fifty years
old. Everything is that old style of heavy old marble and gold
spittons everywhere. And you go—going to the marriage license
place—you go up these real wide marble stairs about a block wide
and sway-backed, you practically break your neck on them they're
so worn down in the middle—and there's this hall upstairs somewhere with the door to the bureau at the far end and by the time
we got there—and we didn't get there till about eleven—there
must have been two hundred people up there waiting in line.
Most of them couples waiting to get in for their license. There
was this line—you've never seen anything like it. We got up to
the top of the stairs and saw all these people in line and Cotton
and me both said, Oh, my God! at the same time. And some of
the kids who had come with us, I thought they'd just drop. You've
never seen anything like it. I wish I could remember some of the
things that our friends said about it, too, because they kept us in
stitches all morning. [*Pause.*] God, you should have seen the
people waiting there in line. It was hot and all. Of course this
was Chicago, but I'll bet it'll be the same, or about the same
everywhere. There was every size and shape and color a person
you've ever seen or could hope to see. God, there was Puerto
Ricans and whites and redheads and Negroes and redheaded
Negroes; and a lot of people were chattering away in some jib-
berish language that nobody could understand. And kids you'd
think was only about fourteen years of age and old people who
must have been—one couple—must have been sixty if they were
a day. You see everything. And this is hard to believe probably
but you can go down to the New York City Hall and I'll bet it's
the same there; I'll swear about twenty of the girls in line waiting
for their marriage licenses were pregnant. Honest to God. It looked
like the maternity ward in a hospital. And I mean real pregnant
—six or seven months along—and I couldn't help thinking if this
many are this pregnant this far along, I just wonder how many
are three months or two months along and nobody can tell it.

And of course there were some mothers and fathers that had dragged along. If you ever want to see a trapped look in a boy's eyes— I mean, they were smiling, and talking all very seriously with their prospective fathers-in-law, all very man to man, standing beside their fat, ugly—really ugly, some of them—girl friends, and in their eyes they were wondering how the hell they were going to get out of this one. And some of the girls were dressed up. Some of them were in jeans and had their hair in curlers and you'd just want to die looking at them—and then some of them were dressed to the teeth. Knee-length wedding gowns; you know; not expensive, but pretty and veils and the whole bit—a bunch of roses or gardenias or something and after they got their license they went around a kind of mezzanine railing to the Justice's office across the way. The Justice of the Piece's office some of the kids started calling it. That's the kind of thing they were saying all day. But if I was going to wear a dress like that to get married in, I know one thing: I wouldn't do it in his little office—you could look right across into the room and the carpet was worn all down—it was just a mess of a place. I couldn't even watch— I just bet they felt so foolish all dressed up like that with this noisy line outside and that stupid rug. But they seemed happy enough about it, I guess. You couldn't help wondering if the boys who were marrying the pregnant girls were really the fathers of the kids or not. And if the boys weren't wondering the same thing. I just hope that all the kids turned out for the mothers' sake to look exactly the spittin' image of their fathers.

And if this hot, messy, stupid crowd wasn't enough, with everyone crowding all over this hall: there was this guy, all fat and toothless, or nearly, and bald, who kept trotting down the line saying, "Stay up against the wall, now, give the boys room to get in. They got you up against the wall now; now you let them in!" And pretending what he'd said didn't have any dirty meaning at all. And laughing. Some of the fellows and the men —the fathers and all—laughed and carried on with him. I can't remember exactly what he said but it was like: "The quicker you get in the quicker you get it in." I mean he just wasn't funny at all. I thought Cotton was gonna bust him one. He just *served* to make everyone a little more nervous and jumpy than they were anyway. Everyone got so tired and just kept looking and everyone was so down. Naturally the girls who were pregnant were mostly just looking down at the hall floor, and they'd look up like nothing was wrong. I guess everyone just wanted to get the hell out of that building. I know I thought, *Christ, aren't we even moving? You know?* With, let's see, with Cotton and me there was two friends of his that I didn't know too well, and a girl friend of mine, so we weren't as bad off as the kids that had come down there alone. Not at first. We were talking and cutting up and all. And after a while you get so tired and exhausted you just stand there. And everyone was more stupid and ugly than you can imagine and Cotton got in one of his moods. You know: quiet as a stone statue or something and I tried to get him out of it. It was like he blamed *me* for all the waiting and all. And then when we finally got in, after creeping along all afternoon, there was three tables and after we got inside the room the line split into three lines and we went to one of the tables—and the guy who asked the questions—real crazy questions too, but I can't remember any of them now. I should, too, because they were such crazy questions. This guy was friendly and nice and Cotton became hisself again, which was about time. Anyway that guy was nice and friendly, considering he'd been doing the same thing all morning with one couple after another. And all the guys joked kinna dirty, but friendly and we finally got the license and they had the certificate from the blood test and all; and we went back out to the kids that waited for us. They were sitting on the steps, just about to die it looked like. I don't know how they did it. But a lot of the couples were worse off than we were—there seemed like thousands of them still hanging around up there when we left. Elizabeth—that was the girl friend of mine who came along, stood out on the front steps there with the license and read it out—every word. Outloud. And everyone was laughing and carrying on. Christ, they were a fun gang. They were about the most fun kids I've ever been with in my life. And let's see; we went for a drive, trying to cool off, I remember. And I don't know, we probably went to a drive-in movie, out somewhere. We were always doing that because Harold had his car. And when we got home I put the license on the dresser, stood it up so we could look at it. Cotton said if we'd all been getting two dollars an hour the thing was worth about thirty dollars, I'll bet. [*Pause.*] When had we decided to get *married?* I think at first we were going to do it the next day—Sunday, but we'd been out all night that night and by the time we got up that Sunday it must have been seven or eight o'clock in the evening. And then we were going to do it the next week. And, I don't know—something came up —one thing or another. Cotton was out a lot, but he still came over and all, and he still wanted to and so did I. I really did. I wanted to more than anything because he was about the greatest guy I'd ever met. And I don't know. I know one time when I was trying to straighten up the place—trying to get a little order out of my room, I put it in one of the dresser drawers and it finally got buried under a pile of stuff. I've got it though, I ran across it again when I was packing things together to come here. Hell, old Cotton had cut out months before that. He kept coming over for a long time, but I might not be able to tell when a guy isn't really interested in me at first—I mean if they just say they are, I believe them—I mean what else can you do? But I can sure as hell tell when they start losing interest. Not that you can do anything about it. Old Cotton would give me a kiss and squeeze me once and slap me three or four times quick on the rump. And say, "Okay!" like I was dismissed or something. Like he had better things to run and do at that particular moment, or he had thoughts; like he was preoccupied at the moment. "Okay! Hop up!" Hop up. Good Lord.

But he hadn't chickened out of it—getting married—he just never got around to it. I've sometimes wished we just had gone out of town, out to Glen Ellyn or somewhere at a Justice of the Peace, somewhere. You know. It just got to be such a mess we never even talked about it after a while, and the license got shuffled up with a lot of other things, and got a bend across it, all bent up. He was a nice guy, too. He moved on back South somewhere. Georgia, I think. Not Alabama, I know. And he'd had a lot of great friends, too. I liked them a lot. God, did we ever have some *times* together. The whole . . . gang of us. God. We used . . . to really have some . . . times together.

The quartette is together at the back of the stage. They harmonize in a rock'n'roll wordless "Boo, bop, boo, bah, day, dolie, olie day" kind of rambling that gets louder and eventually takes over the scene. FRANK *has left;* JOHN *is in the café now.* JOE *and* DOPEY *and* RAKE *have gone to the corner.* DAVID *and* FRANNY *enter the café.*

DAVID. Hi, John; you got any coffee?
JOHN. Sure.
FRANNY. Two.

DARLENE *looks in her purse for money.*

ANN. I'll get it.

DARLENE. No, that's okay.

ANN. It's okay. Sam couldn't possibly miss a quarter.

FRANNY. Do you have a menu in this place? For Chris' sake.

XAVIER *and* BABE *enter.* BABE *is not high but is so far gone that you couldn't tell it. She speaks very thickly and to the floor and it should be just barely possible to understand her. Their scene should be played on the street, some distance from the corner, very slowly.*

JOHN [*to* FRANNY]. Hold it a minute. [*To* ANN.] Thanks.

ANN *and* DARLENE *remain in the café for a moment.*

XAVIER [*to* JOE]. Hey, friend.

JOE. *Xavier!* What are you doing?

XAVIER. Where was you yesterday?

JOE. Oh, I was busy. Where you going?

XAVIER. You want to come up?

JOE [*looks at* BABE, *nods.* BABE *stares blankly at him*]. Where you going?

BABE. Come on, Xavier.

XAVIER. We're going up on the roof a minute.

RAKE [*from the other side, singing to himself*]. They laugh and jab, cavort, and jump!——

DOPEY. Shut up. For Chris' sake.

RAKE. What's wrong?

JOE. No, I been up there. What for?

DOPEY. You get on my nerves.

BABE [*to* XAVIER]. Haven't you got one? A something?

XAVIER. We've got to go on up.

ERNESTO *joins* DOPEY *and* RAKE.

BABE. Come on. You have to have something. You used to have a cord or something, didn't you?

XAVIER. Yeah, someone borrowed it, didn't give it back.

BABE [*looks at* JOE's *belt*]. Uh, do you think I, would you. . . .

JOE *slips off his belt, rolls it up, and hands it to* XAVIER.

ANN. I just wonder where the fuck Sam's run off to.

BABE. Good, great. That's thin, that's fine.

JOE. I'll see you when you come down. Don't lose that.

XAVIER [*rather shyly*]. Come on up.

JOE. No, I'll see you when you come down. Don't lose that.

XAVIER. I'll bring it right back. We'll see you.

JOE. Yeah, look; I'm not staying around here long, I might be inside when you come down, okay?

XAVIER. Sure, man. We'll be right back. You should come along.

JOE. You go on. [XAVIER *and* BABE *exit*.] Jesus, Xavier.

The quartette sings the first four or five lines of "There Is a Balm in Gilead" in the back, a jazzed-up version.

DARLENE [*comes out of the café. Sees* JOE *and goes to him. Their scene is played on the street corner*]. Hi.

JOE. Hi. You been calling over to your room for me?

DARLENE. No, you said not to. Why, has the phone been ringing?

JOE. Yeah. It's probably Chuckles. I don't imagine it took him much to discover who I was with the last few nights. You being new and all.

DARLENE. Almost everyone I've seen all day asked me where you was.

JOE. Yeah? What'd you say?

DARLENE [*smiles*]. I told them I thought you went to a movie.

JOE. Really? That's pretty good. That's funny. Say, you know Xavier?

DARLENE. Sure. Someone was looking for him.

JOE. I saw him. Pushing now. I'll bet he has been all along. He was with Babe.

DARLENE. Babe? Really? [*She has no idea what to say*.]

JOE. I'm not going to.

DARLENE. Not what?

JOE. I'm not going to. I decided not.

DARLENE. Really? Oh, God, I'm glad, Joe. Oh, I really am. How are you gonna do it?

JOE. I gotta think of some way to get these back to Perry or Chuckles. I'll just give him what he gave me and tell him I've changed my mind.

FRANNY *enters.*

DARLENE. Oh, I'm glad. I really am. You'll do something else all right.

FRANNY [*on the street opposite the corner*]. Hello, Ernesto.

The quartette begins a very low, highly harmonized version of the hymn "Balm in Gilead" that follows the tempo of JOE *and* DAR-LENE's *slow, rather dreamy scene.*

DARLENE. Did you sleep till six?

ERNESTO [*with deep insinuation, grabbing* FRANNY *around waist*]. You like it?

FRANNY. I'm not really interested, no. [As TIG *joins* DOPEY, FRANNY, RAKE, *and* ERNESTO.] Hi, Tig.

JOE. About six. I didn't get to bed till late.

DARLENE. I know.

TIG [*with hand on crotch*]. You like it, Franny? You think you could use something?

FRANNY. I'll bet you think you're a man. Don't you know——

DARLENE. When are you going to see him?

FRANNY. ——men don't dig boys? They sure don't dig fairies.

TIG. Depends on what it's worth to you.

JOE. I don't know. Soon as I can. I got to call him or something.

DARLENE. When did you decide?

FRANNY. You really think you're hot stuff, don't you?

TIG. How much is it worth to you?

JOE. Just a minute ago.

DARLENE. What'll you do?

JOE. Hell, there's a thousand things to do.

ANN [*exiting the café*]. Franny, you're stealing all my business.

Group laughs.

DARLENE. Sure.

FRANNY [*to* TIG]. You really think you're good enough to charge?

TIG. Five bucks an inch'll get me fifty, Franny?

FRANNY. Who from? Not me.

JOE. When did you wake up?

FRANNY. I'll charge you double.

DARLENE. Since about ten. . . .

TIG. How much can you take?

FRANNY. As much as I need and want.

TIG. Put your money where your mouth is, sweetheart.

Group laughs. TIG *is very close to* FRANNY.

DARLENE. I went down to the bus station. I had some clothes still in a locker there; I thought I'd never get them.

FRANNY. More than you got, sweetheart.

TIG. How do you know?

DOPEY. Watch it, Tig. [*His back is to the audience, hands in pockets.*]

ANN [*turns and goes back inside*]. Watch it, Franny; he'll take you up.

FRANNY. Come on, back off a little bit. I'm only human.

KAY [*entering café*]. Hi, John; I'm a little late.
JOHN. Hi, Kay; that's all right.

FICK enters.

DARLENE [*over some of the above*]. The neighborhood isn't bad **at**
   all in the daytime. It's perfectly respectable.
JOE. Is it?
DARLENE. Well. Nearly.
RAKE. He can take care of himself.
FRANNY. I'll bet I could take care of him better.
TIG. You think you could take about half of that?
FRANNY. Half of what? I don't *see* anything.
RAKE. Watch that one, though, Tig.

Group reaction.

ERNESTO. No lie, Tig.
DARLENE. The people look like anyone else. Almost.
JOE. Almost. That's funny.
TIG. You think you can take about ten bucks' worth, real quick-like?
FICK [*inside the café*]. Hey, John? Am I frostbitten? Look at my **ears.**
JOHN. What?
DOPEY. Why don't you take us all on, huh?
RAKE. Game for that?
FICK. Hey, Ann?
DARLENE. You want a cup of coffee or something?
JOE. In a minute.
FRANNY. No, it's not my game.
DARLENE. I talked to Ann all afternoon.
FRANNY. Sorry, Rake.
JOE. She's a wild kid.
DARLENE. Kid, hell.
FICK. Hell.
ANN. Hell no, you aren't frostbit. It's not even cold out.
FICK. You sure?
FRANNY. It won't be real quick, I can tell you that right now.
FICK. 'Cause I can't tell.
TIG. I'll let you savor it a hour maybe.
KAY. How's business been?
JOHN. Not good, not bad. Coffee, Ann?
FRANNY. Or three. I could give you a ride you won't forget.
ANN. Why not.

TIG. You think so, huh?

JOE. She's nice, I like her.

DARLENE. So do I, really.

DOPEY [*turning his head around. To audience*]. Are you getting any of this?

FICK. Could I have a coffee?

JOHN [*to* FICK]. Are you awake?

FRANNY. How long do you have to hang around your friends here?

FICK. Awake?

TIG. What friends?

RAKE. I don't believe it!

FRANNY. Believe anything, baby.

TIG. What can I tell you?

FICK. What is it, November?

DARLENE. I like her. I talked her leg off.

> JOE *laughs.*

FRANNY. Come on up, you springy son-of-a-bitch.

TIG. You better be all you claim.

ERNESTO. Want a party?

FRANNY. I'm not dressed for it. [*To* TIG.] I'll just bet you got action like a jack rabbit.

TIG. How much is it worth to find out?

FRANNY [*as he and* TIG *start to leave*]. Well, we'll talk about it. Okay?

JOE. You want to go in?

DARLENE. Might as well. I've been in all day, though.

> JOE *and* DARLENE *enter the café.*

RAKE [*to* TIG *and* FRANNY]. Hey, you're gonna lose it, baby.

FRANNY. I never had it.

> *The next four speeches are delivered rapidly over the above.*

ERNESTO. You'll get split open, Franny!

RAKE. Rip him apart.

DOPEY. Give it to her.

ERNESTO. Make him cry for mercy, Tig.

TIG. I'll have him beggin' in five minutes.

FRANNY. Quit bragging and get to work. I'll see you guys later.

Group laughs. The group moves back a few feet. TIG *and* FRANNY **exit.** *The* STRANGER *should be standing where the last line of* FRANNY's *is spoken.*

DOPEY [*to audience*]. Wheeh! Jesus.

ANN [*leaving the café and joining the group*]. Did he do it? The son-of-a-bitch! Damn Franny.

RAKE. You got Sammy.

ANN. Damn Sam. I been trying to make Tig for a month.

ERNESTO. Don't tell Sammy.

ANN. Screw Sammy.

DOPEY. Franny'll end up like old Howie yet.

ANN. Poor old Howie.

> DARLENE *and* JOE *sit in a booth.*

DOPEY. Poor old Howie.

> *Group laughs.*

RAKE. Son-of-a-bitch!

> *Group laughs.*

RAKE. Wire . . . [*Laughs.*]

ANN. God, that's funny. It really is.

During ANN's *following speech the café is filled by the same people as in the beginning scene of the play. Black and orange crêpe-paper streamers are lowered very slowly in a typical crisscross Halloween decoration. A dime-store skeleton and a pumpkin should lower straight from the ceiling. The quartette is rehearsing the opening song in the back.*

ANN [*to audience*]. There's this joke: I can't tell it. Not a joke joke, but like a private joke on this guy Howie from around here.

RAKE [*over, in background*]. Poor old Howie.

ANN. Like the devil gets his due, you understand. See, he's always around and for three or four dollars, I don't know how much, I never bothered to ask, but the guys around here would always pick up a few bucks from Howie. He's not an old guy either, I mean not all that old, but they'd step into a doorway or some dark place along the street or some rest-room, you follow me, and the guys would make about four or five bucks—a symbiotic kind of relationship—you know, the guys get the money and Howie gets, or derives, his benefit from it too: This is sounding vulgar as hell and I thought I could tell it clean. Well, anyway—Fuck. Howie gives them a quickie blow job in a subway john or somewhere—Christ, we're all adult and know about that, I'd hope, by now, anyway. And this is very important to him. Like a junkie needs his shot in the arm. Well, poor Howie, God love him, never hurt anybody, was down in the Village and just out to see the sights, not approaching anyone or anything, at least no more than he could help; just walking around and some guys jump him. Figure him for a good rolling, and maybe they got a few dollars off the guy and left him pretty beaten up but that wouldn't be so bad for Howie, you know—and he made it to the hospital. Over to Saint Vincent's, see, and they gave him X rays and he's got his face knocked in and his teeth loosened; nothing really bad or serious or permanent, you understand. He'll be back in shape in about a month; but in the meantime he's got this broken jaw. . . .

RAKE. Hey, Ann; come on.

ANN. So they wired his mouth shut!

> *Group reaction.* ANN *laughs at her own joke.*

DOPEY. Poor bastard, Howie.

RAKE. Poor Howie.

> *Group laughs.* FICK *exits café.* ANN *re-enters.*

FICK [*as he passes* ANN]. Hey, Ann, you got—hey, you . . .

> *She is gone.*

JUDY. All right! Come on, come on. If we're going to get goin', get goin'; get that table out of the way, come on, line them up a little.

They straighten the booths into rows. Blocking on these repeat scenes should be as the first time through exactly.

TIG [*overlapping*]. What are you? Some kind of housewife, Judy?

JUDY [*to* DAVID]. You're the housewife, aren't you, sweetheart?

DAVID. You're the fishwife, Judy. Fishwife! Fish! Pheew!

FICK. Hey, Dopey, you got a cigarette, huh?

DOPEY. Somewhere.

BONNIE [*to* DAVID]. You ought to be chased out of the neighborhood. Dirty up the neighborhood with a lot of fairy dust.

DAVID [*not* FRANNY, *this time*]. Who you calling names, you truck driver?

BONNIE. Who you queers think you are?

DAVID. Who you callin' queer? George!

BOB. Shut up, over there!

JOHN [*not* TIG]. Come on, God.

TERRY. All you queens.

DAVID [*to* TERRY]. Why don't you shut up before I beat you over your head with your dildo?

TERRY. You trying to say something?

DAVID. Ah, your mother's a whore——

TERRY. You trying to say something?

FOUR CHILDREN, *three boys and a girl, enter the scene. They are dressed in regular clothes; they all have on Halloween masks. The boys wear comical masks; the girl a woman's mask. They carry big paper bags and go about saying "trick or treat." No one in the café pays the slightest attention to them. The scene is repeated as though they weren't there. All new material is ignored by the others.*

JOHN. Come on, now; keep it down.

TIM. May I have a cup of tea, please? [CARLO *enters.*] Hi, Carlo. Over here.

CARLO [*trying English*]. Hello. Correct? Yes, hello. Correct?

TIM [*with Spanish accent*]. Correct. Near enough. [*The next few lines will be over the repeat below, beginning with* BONNIE'S *speech; but they should be loud and excited.*] Try the numbers, though. That's what you're working on.

CARLO. Numbers. No. [*Quickly counts to ten—as a joke—in Spanish.*]

TIM. No. No. No. In English. In English. How you ever gonna learn anything?

ANN. He'll never get it anyway.

CARLO. Yes!

TIM. Yes, he will. You wait.

BONNIE. What the hell is this, fifty cents for one Coke; you think this is the Ritz?

JOHN. There's a sign right there, fifty cents minimum at booths; if you don't have it, don't sit there.

FICK [*on the corner, to* DOPEY]. Hey, ain't we seen this once?

DOPEY. It's important.

A CHILD. Trick or treat!?

FICK. They're new!

DOPEY. Shut up, for Chris' sake.

BONNIE. Screw it; I'm paying no fifty cents for one Coke.

KAY [*to* JOHN]. Toast with that.

BOB. Fifty cents you can get a good high.

BONNIE. Gimme a grilled cheese, hell, if I'm going to spend a fortune. One goddamned Coke.

KAY. And a jack.

BONNIE. Christ, you'd think this place was the Ritz!

DAVID [to BOB]. Come on up to my room. It won't kill you.

ANN. It won't kill you, Bob.

STRANGER [enters and comes to JOE]. Hi again.

JOE. I don't know you.

BOB. Knock it off.

DAVID. Come on up with me, it won't hurt you.

BOB [to ANN]. How much scratch? Jack? Tonight?

ANN. None of your damn business. Ask Sammy, you want to know.

JOHN. You still keepin' that bum? What's he do with all that dough?

ANN. He banks it. Or at least he'd better be banking it.

BOB. Yeah, he banks it with Cameron or Chuckles.

ANN. He don't truck with that junk. He'd better not; I'd crack him over the head.

DOPEY *has turned to the audience as the* STRANGER *first spoke.*
DOPEY'S *speech is over the scene in the café. He speaks to the audience, quite casually.*

DOPEY. See, what happened, the whole thing—Joe's a nice guy; he really is, but you bum around and you bum around and you start to wonder just how the hell you're going to ever get out of it; and you think if you could get in a good position—if you could get in with Chuckles. See, there's a lot of dough being made around. And he figured he'd have some of it. But see, he really didn't like the idea, the risk, of pushing, so he wasn't tough enough for it. And it's as simple as that. And Chuckles is big. These guys are big, some of them. Those boys are about as powerful as anyone in the country, I guess, and you don't cross them is the thing. It isn't done. Everything would have been okay, but, see, Joe didn't know till a few days ago that he didn't want to go in with Chuckles. And Chuckles just naturally thought that Joe was holding out on him. Now for once he was patient. He sent a fellow to tell Joe to shape up. You saw that all right. And he tried to protect his investment. But even for once is a rare thing with Chuckles and Joe just didn't let him *know*. Now Chuckles is a big guy around here. He bleeds these guys around here. He can't have them see him made a fool of. And he gave Joe time. [*This last is almost screamed over the scene in the back.*]

FICK [to DOPEY]. He did, that's true. That's true as can be. He wouldn't do that for me.

DOPEY [*still to audience*]. So now they're gonna kill him.

FICK. Joe?

DOPEY. Yeah.

FICK. We ain't seen this, have we?

DOPEY *shakes his head, quietly; mouths, "No." They turn toward the stage to watch.*

STRANGER [*this follows* ANN's *last line before* DOPEY's *speech to the audience: some of it will be covered by the end of* DOPEY's *speech. He takes a cattle syringe from his pocket*]. You ever see one of these?

JOE. What?

STRANGER. One of these?

JOE. A syringe? Christ, look at the size of it. What is it, a works for elephants? [*He laughs.*]

STRANGER. For livestock. For cattle and pigs.

JOE. You don't use something like that. That's too fancy. You use a works. An eye dropper, a piece of dollar.* A needle.

TIM [*to* CARLO]. One, two, three, four, five.

STRANGER. You do, huh?

CARLO. No. No.

TIM. Slow then. One. Come on. One.

A CHILD. Trick or treat.

JOHN. Get out of here, you kids, go on.

STRANGER. You do, huh?

JOE. They do. Why do you show me that?

ANN [*to* TIM]. He'll never get it.

CARLO. One!

TIM [*not too loudly*]. Bravo.

JOE [*over*]. I've got no use for it.

DARLENE [*to* JOE]. What's wrong?

TIM. Two. Come on.

JOE [*to* DARLENE]. Nothing.

STRANGER. Chuckles wanted you to know what hit you. Understand? That's a four-inch reach. You don't screw Chuckles. Understand?

JOE [*stands. To* STRANGER]. I got something to tell him.

DARLENE. What? What is it?

JOE. No! Come on.

* A junkie seldom uses a syringe. He uses an eye-dropper, attached to a surgical needle with a thin piece of paper rolled around the needle, serving as a gasket. For paper they often use a thin strip torn from the edge of a dollar bill.

JOHN [*to the* CHILDREN]. Go on, scram. Get out of here. Scram out of here. Go on!

Dim on café. Spot on JOE *and* STRANGER. STRANGER *reaches back and stabs* JOE *underhanded in the heart.*

BOB. God!

TERRY. Jesus!

DARLENE [*over*]. No!

Simultaneously, the CHILDREN *run out with the paper sacks flapping over their heads. They are screaming and yelling joyously. They split and two go one way, two another. They circle around the café and enter from the back and run through again. Lights up on café.*

THE SCENE IS REPEATED.

JOHN. Go on, scram. Get out of here. Scram out of here. Go on!

Dim on café. Spot on JOE *and* STRANGER. *The* STRANGER *stabs* JOE *as before.*

BOB. God!

TERRY. Jesus!

DARLENE [*over*]. No!

The CHILDREN *run out and circle the café as before. Lights up on café.*

THE SCENE IS REPEATED.

JOHN. Go on, scram. Get out of here. Scram out of here. Go on!

Dim on café. Spot on JOE *and* STRANGER. *The* STRANGER *stabs* JOE.

BOB. God!

TERRY. Jesus!

The CHILDREN *run through the café.*

JOE [*pulls a number of white packets from his pockets and spills them all over the stage in front of him*]. I don't want them. I don't want it! Take them! Take them back! I don't want them!

The CHILDREN *split in twos and run off screaming.*

DARLENE [*over screaming*]. No, no, no, no!

The STRANGER *runs off.* JOE *falls among* BOB, TERRY, ANN, CARLO, *and* TIM. JOE *is taken behind the counter, away, out of sight of the audience. Not hidden, but removed from audience's sight. There is a time lapse. No one mentions the stabbing.* DARLENE *sits through this scene without comment or without looking up.*

TIG [*instantly, as soon as* JOE *falls.* FRANK *is behind the counter now*]. What the hell are you talking about. . . .

FRANK. Why don't you stop coming in here, you don't——

TIG. What the hell, you're trying to screw——

FRANK [*cutting in*]. Get on out now.

TIG. You trying to cheat me outta four bucks, baby, you can't pull——

FRANK. I never cheat you outta nothing.

TERRY [*over, to* DAVID]. You queers just sit down, take it easy.

TIG. I gave you a five, a five, you son of——

FRANK. You get on out of here.

TIG. You want to step outside? You want to step out from behind that counter, baby? You watch it, Frank.

JOHN [*cutting in*]. Come on, Tig, give up, go on out.

FRANK. Get out of this place.

TIM. Try again.

ANN. He's not gonna get it, I know.

CARLO. Yes.

TIG. Ah, come on, I gave him a five, man, you know what he's trying.

JOHN. Come on, go on, Tig.

CARLO. One.

JOHN. Come on, go on, Tig.

TIG [*leaving*]. You wait, Frank; you'll get yours, buddy.

FRANK [*after* TIG *has gone*]. Get on out of here, bum!

TIG [*yelling back heatedly*]. All right, now, goddammit I'm out, you just shut your mouth, Frank; you stupid bastard. Buddy, you're really gonna get it one day, Frank, and I want to be there to watch it. You're gonna get your head split open, dumb bastard.

FICK [*very clearly during the fray, to* DOPEY, *who ignores the question*]. Hey, where's Joe?

RUST [*running in to café*]. Hey, they got Jerry Joe in the can!

BOB. Jerry the fairy?

DAVID. You watch who you're calling names.

RUST. He tried to put the make on a cop.

BOB. They gonna book him?

RUST. Whatta you mean? He tried to put the make on a cop. Hell, yes, they'll book him. He had eight bombinos on him! Man, are they hot for that stuff.

General crowd reaction.

Tim. She's right, you'll never learn.

Carlo. *Sí*—no, yes! I will.

Tim. Say, "Yes, I will."

Carlo. Yes, I will.

> *General crowd murmur to themselves during this.*

Tim. You're getting the wrong damn accent. Just repeat it. Take it slow. You'll learn.

Ann. Not a chance, Timmy. He's never learned anything.

Tim. He will. One.

Carlo [*repeating rapidly*]. One.

Tim. Two.

Carlo. Two.

Tim. Three.

Carlo. Three.

Tim. Four.

Carlo. Four.

Tim. Five.

Carlo. Fife.

Tim. Five, Carlo; five, five!

Carlo [*overlapping*]. Yes, I know. Five.

Tim. Good, six.

Carlo. Six.

> *On "six" the quartette enters with a downbeat as at the beginning,*
> *singing the first five bars of the rock'n'roll song.*

Tim. Come on!

Ann [*loudly breaking it up*]. No. Stop it! No, stop it. You can't do it that way. It isn't right.

> *They stop, wander off for a retake.*

Ann [*apologetically*]. It's just not it, you know—not right.

> *During* Ann's *speech* Tim *and* Carlo *have begun counting again.*
> *They reach "seven" and the quartette returns as before with as*
> *much of the song.* Ann *and* John *shout them down. Everyone is*
> *wandering about aimlessly.*

Ann [*to quartette*]. No, come on. Stop it.

Terry [*to quartette*]. Knock it off—come on.

Ann [*to* John]. It's just not the way to end it.

> *Quartette exits as before.*

John. I *know*. Try to tell them something. God.

TIM *and* CARLO *have started over again.* DOPEY, RAKE, *and* BOB
have run up to stop the quartette.

TIM. Four.
CARLO. Four.
TIM. Five.
CARLO. Five.
TIM. Good, six.
CARLO. Six.
TIM. Seven.
CARLO. Seven.
TIM. Eight.
CARLO. Eight.
TIM. Nine.
CARLO. Nine.
TIM. Ten.
CARLO. Ten.
TIM. Good!

At "ten" DOPEY, RAKE, *and* BOB *begin their round, downstage center. This time not as a round, but all singing softly and liltingly.*

> They laugh and jab
> cavort and jump
> and joke and gab
> and grind and bump.
>
> They flip a knife
> and toss a coin
> and spend their life
> and scratch their groin
>
> They pantomime
> a standing screw
> and pass the time
> with nought to do.
>
> They swing, they sway
> this cheerful crew,
> with nought to say
> and nought to do.

*The cast hums the tune very softly. During the song the crêpe-paper
and Halloween decorations ascend slowly. Everyone in the café picks*

*up the "set" as before and slowly walks the set back toward its
original position. BABE walks, as before, beside the others, not carrying the set. The lights dim slowly at the beginning of DOPEY, RAKE,
and BOB's song.*

FICK [*over the singing, cued by TIM's "Good!" He is wandering
about the stage as at the beginning.*] Hey, buddy, hey, fellow . . .
hey, you got a cigarette on you? Hey . . . Hey, Ann? Uh, cold,
huh? Uh, Dopey, you got . . . Hey . . . Hey . . .

*The song has finished. Several continue to hum. Everyone sets the
"set" back in its original place and takes a position similar to the
beginning, only FICK is sitting at a table and DARLENE and ANN are
at the counter, backs to audience. The lights hold at about half.*

RAKE [*to no one, looking at no one*]. You travel around, I mean a
hustler travels around. . . .

DOPEY [*to no one, to himself*]. And they cut down, through one
century to the one before that, and the one before that. . . .

FICK [*at the booth, to himself*]. You know what I mean? You know
what I mean? . . . You know what I mean? . . . I mean. . . .

DARLENE [*to ANN, very slow, tired, after a kind of sigh*]. And, I don't
know. Everyone was so tired and so down, and I thought, Christ,
aren't we even moving? You know?

The lights have faded out.

Curtain.

LUDLOW FAIR

A Play in One Act

CHARACTERS

RACHEL, *an attractive young woman in her mid-twenties.*

AGNES, *on the heavy side, busty, not unattractive, but no raving beauty, in her mid-twenties. She would be considered "a great deal of fun."*

SCENE: The bedroom of their apartment. Two twin beds on one wall, a vanity dresser across the room. A desk with books. The room is neat and in good taste. On the table between the beds is a phone. On the desk, is a dictionary, among other books; on the vanity is, among the usual paraphernalia, a box of large hair rollers and a bottle of nail polish. One exit is to the bathroom, another to the living room. RACHEL wears a gown and robe; AGNES, pajamas and robe.

Ludlow Fair was first presented by Joe Cino at the Caffe Cino, New York City, on February 1, 1965. It was directed by Neil Flanagan with the following cast:

| RACHEL | Martha Galphin |
| AGNES | Jennie Ventriss |

Lighting by Dennis Parichy, sets by Mr. Flanagan. Stage manager Renée Mauguin.

LUDLOW FAIR

RACHEL [*wandering around the room alone. She is restless; she looks at one thing and another. Finally, quite to herself*]. Oh, God; I think you're losing your head. I think you're going stark raving insane and you've got no one in this ever-loving world, sweetheart, to blame except yourself. And maybe Joe. But then. . . . Are you losing it? Hmm? Let's see. [*She pinches herself firmly. For a full two seconds she considers the effect. Matter-of-factly.*] Ouch! [*Yelling toward the bathroom.*] Agnes? [*Waits.*] How long are you going to take, anyway?

AGNES [*offstage, from the bathroom*]. What?

RACHEL. I said, are you about through in there?

AGNES. In a minute.

RACHEL. You said that an hour ago. [*She waits for an answer, none comes. Rubbing her arm.*] What a stupid thing to do. That's no kind of test of insanity, anyway. That's for drunkenness or sleepwalking or disorderly conduct or something. How do you know if your faculties are ebbing away from you, anyway? [*Seriously considering.*] You go to an analyst, what does he do? You lie down on the couch, what does he do? Ha! No, a respectable analyst, what does he do? You lie—— A quick little word association. You can't give yourself a word—well, why not? [*Sits quickly on the chair at the desk.*] Ready? Ready. Very well, when I say a word you come in with the very first word that pops into your head. Yes, I understand. Very well. [*Pause, tries for a split second to think of a word. Finally.*] Word. [*Immediately answers.*] Word! [*Blank pause.*] Dog. [*Absolutely blank for the count of six. Aside.*] Oh, for Christ's sake. . . . [*Intense concentration. Mumbles.*] Dog. [*Breaking away, then firmly.*] Jesus Chri—DOG! [*Pause. With the same studied intensity.*] CAT! [*Aside.*] For Christ's sake— well, that's it—cat. Keep it up. Cat. [*Same amount of pause between words, same intensity to each word.*] Rat. Mouse. House. Rat. Dog. Cat. Mouse. Louse. Bat. Pat. Fat. Louse. [*Breaking away.*] Fat louse, Jesus Christ. Rat, cat, mouse, louse, bat, house; you don't need an analyst you need an exterminator. You can't associate with yourself. Even words. [*Calling to no one.*] Joe! [*Sees *the dictionary on the desk, puts it in her lap.*] Well, why not? As long as you don't know the word that's coming up. Now the first word that pops into your head. [*Answering herself.*] Yes, I understand. [*She opens the book, looks down, closes it. Flatly.*] Knickerbocker! [*Sighs slowly, then with redetermination.*] All right, I'll play your stupid game with you. Holiday. Take that. [*Opens the book again. Looks more closely. Reading.*] Phen-a-kis-to-scope. [*Pause. Looking at it. Continues reading.*] "An instrument resembling the zoe-thrope in principle and use. One form consists of a disk with the figures arranged about the center, with radial slits—— [*Aside.*] Radial slits? [*Continues to read.*] Radial slits through which the figures are viewed—[*Becoming amused.*]—by means of a mirror." [*Closing the dictionary.*] But what's it *for*? Phen-a-kis-to-scope. Very well. [*She gets up, wanders to the dresser. As though she were thinking.*] Phenakistoscope. Ah, ah . . . Zoethrope! Naturally. [*Sitting at the dresser, the dictionary open in front of her, she quite casually opens the nail polish and pours an amount on one page, shuts the dictionary firmly, props it open again, like an easel against the back of the vanity. Studies it carefully from some distance.*] Ah . . . Oh, ah . . . A tree. [*Aside.*] A tree. That couldn't possibly mean anything. [*Looks back at it, studying.*] Ah. Ah. Your trouble is you have no imagination, Rachel. You're not nuts, you're just dull. Okay . . . Ah. An ostrich. That's a little better. An ostrich. Eating. [*Considering her progress.*] An ostrich, huh? That's vaguely phallic, you know. Well, vaguely. [*Shutting the book.*] That's the trouble with those things, when they start working you're in trouble. [*She gets up, carrying the book, rubs her arm.*] If you don't learn to stop pinching yourself. [*Calling.*] Agnes? Are you ever getting out of there?

AGNES [*offstage*]. What? I'll be out in a minute. Christ.

RACHEL. You said that an hour ago. [*She lays the book back on the dresser, wanders about.*] There's nothing wrong with you, Rachel, except you're given to talking to yourself—*driven* to talking to yourself. [*Falls down on her bed, stretched out, looking up blankly.*] Long pointless conversations before retiring. Well, doctor—it's this way. Joe turned out to be a rat. But then I think I knew that before he turned out. [*Props herself on one elbow.*] I was just sitting home saying to myself, Rachel, you have *got* to get yourself a new phenakistoscope. The one you've got is just a mess. The radial slits are all shot. And when the radial slits are shot, there's just no hope. For a phenakistoscope. Or anything else, for that matter. [*She sits on the side of the bed, face in hands, near the point of crying for just a second, then pulls out of it and gets up.*] Oh dear, oh dear, oh dear, oh dear. Joe. Joe. Joe. Where did you go? [*Pause*]. All the way to . . . [*Breaks off. Walks to dresser, sees dictionary.*] What have you been doing? Testing your sanity again, huh? What are you crazy or something? There's nothing wrong with you. [*Sees her reflection in the mirror. Pleased but critical.*] Five foot two. Five foot six, actually: Girls are bigger than ever. Lovely dark hair, fine hair. Opalescent skin. Lovely hips. Fine breasts. Nice legs. Nice, hell, great legs. Not bad ears; good hands. Slightly blah eyes, frankly; but then you can't have everything. [*Echo, breaking away. To herself.*] Can't have everything. What you are is probably a louse. A fool, of course, and a probable louse. Moral to a fault. And where you are a probable louse, Joe is a first-class, A-one definite louse without a doubt, and it is good to have a first-class definite louse out of your hair. [*She lights a cigarette.*] Four hundred and thirty-six dollars. [*Takes a puff; exhales.*] And thirty-eight cents. [*Wandering about.*] And several Government checks, like thirty, say. And about twenty-odd forgeries, and about four cars, and four hundred and thirty-six dollars and thirty-eight cents.

AGNES [*offstage*]. I'm out. What are you up to?

RACHEL [*without paying attention. To herself*]. Oh, God. [*Sees herself in the mirror.*] Girl, you are a mess. Just a mess. [*Pause.*]

AGNES *enters. Without looking directly at* RACHEL, *she goes to her bed, picking up the dictionary on her way and tossing it on her bed.* AGNES *has a cold. She is carrying a box of Kleenex, a section of the* Times *folded open to the crossword, a pencil, a brush and comb, and anything else she can find. Her hair is wet, combed straight down.*

RACHEL [*to herself*]. Well, what do you expect with last year's phenakistoscope?

AGNES [*without looking up, goes to her bed*]. Are you going to take a bath or what?

RACHEL. Take a bath? When did you start saying, "take a bath"? Take a bath, take a haircut, take a shower—I don't know what you're coming to.

AGNES. I got a cold.

RACHEL. What's that got to do with anything?

AGNES. Well, I abbreviate when I got a cold.

She situates herself on the bed with the paraphernalia about her, including a dish of peanut brittle.

RACHEL [*musing sadly*]. Four hundred and thirty-six dollars.

AGNES. [*without looking up from the paper and brushing her hair*]. And thirty-eight cents.

RACHEL. I just wish I knew if I did the right thing.

AGNES. Look. A guy robs a store. If you turn him in, are you doing the right thing?

RACHEL. Do I know this guy or not?

AGNES. What guy?

RACHEL. Who robbed the store. In your hypothesis.

AGNES. Leave my hypothesis out of it. What difference does it make? He robbed a store—you turn him in.

RACHEL. He didn't rob a store.

AGNES. Are you going to take a bath or what?

RACHEL. I don't think so.

AGNES. You going to stay up and read all night or what?

RACHEL. Four hundred bucks. God.

AGNES. If you're going to start brooding I'm going to bed.

RACHEL. If just once we'd say to ourselves—you do that, girl, and you'll be sorry for it later.

AGNES. Yeah. Not bloody likely. [*Blowing her nose.*] Jesus, I'm coming down with something.

RACHEL [*studying her*]. You know what you are?

AGNES. Yeah? Make it good.

RACHEL. Susceptible.

AGNES. Susceptible. You hook the dud and I'm susceptible. I got a lousy job in lousy Kew Gardens and a lousy date tomorrow for lunch and a lousy dentist appointment and a lousy boss and a lousy love life and a roommate who takes out her aggressions on me. And all you can say is I'm susceptible. I'm dying. Face it, Agnes, you got a lousy life.

RACHEL. I meant susceptible to colds. Or drafts.

AGNES. "Agnes Mulligan: This Is Your Life!" And the TV screen goes blank for thirty minutes.

RACHEL. Why do you always have a cold? You've had a cold since I've known you.

AGNES. Maybe I'm allergic to you. I wear low-cut dresses is why. I

knew when I was nine, with a name like Agnes, I was in for a
dumpy figure and a big bust and low-cut dresses and susceptibility
to drafts.

RACHEL. Well, don't wear them.

AGNES [*almost always speaks as if she is talking to herself*]. If I'da
had any brains I'd have changed my name.

RACHEL. Why don't you?

AGNES. What's the point of having a big bust if you don't wear low-
cut dresses. [*She puts the crossword on her lap, picks up the
dictionary. Then, almost dreamily.*] What I can't wait for is a big
house and about six handmaids and a big bed to sprawl all over.
You know . . . I want to keep my figure—what there is of it.
After I'm married, I mean. I really do. I want to look as nice as
possible. God, I think that's important.

RACHEL. Oh, would you shut up?

AGNES [*has opened the dictionary absently during the last speech.
She shuts it and looks at* RACHEL]. What the hell did you do to
the dictionary?

RACHEL. Oh. I made a Rorschach.

AGNES [*pause*]. Yeah.

RACHEL. I was checking my responses. What does it look like to
you?

AGNES [*reopening the dictionary, unamused*]. It looks like I better
know the meaning and derivation of all the possible words between "obsecrate" and "ocelot."

RACHEL. What does it look like, though? Do you get an ostrich?

AGNES. I don't get anything except mad. Jesus, Rachel.

RACHEL. I'm sorry.

AGNES [*pause*]. Good Lord. Nail polish, huh?

RACHEL. Yeah. I thought maybe I was going insane.

AGNES. And the simple act of pouring nail polish into the dictionary
didn't confirm anything, huh?

RACHEL. Don't pester me. Do I eat peanut brittle in bed? I thought
you'd never get out of that tub. Don't you know not to leave a
screwed-up girl alone with herself for three-quarters of an hour?

*She has said it comically, but suddenly feels sad, puts her head in
her hands again.*

AGNES. Well, I was soaking. [*Notices her.*] Aw, come on, for Christ's
sake.

RACHEL. I only want to know if I did the right thing.

AGNES. Look, a hundred of that was mine. He was a bum, what can I tell you? He was a bum and a thief and you turned him into the Secret Service and now what are you conjuring up? Lonely Joe in a cell? Well, forget it.

RACHEL. You're not funny.

AGNES. He was a bum. [*Aside.*] Damn, I'm all over peanut brittle.

RACHEL. He was. Of course he was. But I had no idea he'd done any of that other.

AGNES. How long had you known him?

RACHEL. Three months.

AGNES. Well in three months you're supposed to know everything about the guy? Every bank he's robbed, for Christ's sake?

RACHEL. He hadn't robbed any banks.

AGNES. Federal bank notes passed totaling into the hundreds; you want to get technical, he's robbed a bank. A Federal bank at that. So you had fun; it wasn't worth it.

RACHEL. You're a lot of help. I think I'm going over the edge and you sit there complacently sticking to the blanket.

AGNES [*trying to wipe the blanket and Kleenex off her hands*]. This damn stuff. I'm growing fuzz.

She sets the dish of candy on the table.

RACHEL. What will they do to him, do you think?

AGNES [*quickly, disgruntled*]. I think they'll hang him.

RACHEL [*getting up*]. Stop it! Now you just stop it!

AGNES. Hey, come on. He'll go to jail. He stole my dough and your dough and the Federal Government's dough and God knows whose else's dough and he'll go to jail.

RACHEL. I just couldn't believe it.

AGNES. Yeah, me too.

RACHEL. We really had fun, too.

AGNES. Well, don't think about it, okay?

RACHEL. We really did.

AGNES. She says we really had fun, I tell her don't think about it, she says we really had fun. Jesus. Listen. You know what happened to the fag bookkeeper sits next to me out at work? He picked up this guy. . . .

RACHEL. Agnes, I do not care what happened to the fag bookkeeper out at Standard Universal Plumbing.

AGNES. Standard Universal Fixtures. [*Pause. Firmly.*] There is no such thing as plumbing any more. [*Pause. Continuing.*] He took this guy he'd met up to——

RACHEL. Really! I don't——

AGNES. Look, do you think I'd trouble you if it wasn't pertinent? I'm not in the habit of telling you bedtime stories for the hell of it, am I? He picked up, good Lord, this guy! Apparently they just wander around till they see eye to eye with someone and then run right off the street and hit the sack, which, if you want to know my opinion, sounds a little capricious but not altogether impractical. Anyway, this big lug went home with him and "Stars Fell on Alabama," I suppose, or whatever the hell happens. Anyway, the next morning Henry waves good-by and two days later he sees this doll's picture in the paper—he'd been picked up for murder, my dear, of four or five fairies out in California and God knows how many more between here and there. Poor Henry almost died. He'd spent the night with this guy.

RACHEL [*pause*]. Fine! I'm sorry, I don't see the connection.

AGNES. You said you really had fun and you couldn't believe that Joe could possibly be——

RACHEL. ——We happened to have been going together for three months!——

AGNES. ——And you didn't know a damn thing about him——

RACHEL. You think a one night fling is the same——

AGNES. And you'd had some fun and you didn't know beans about him——

RACHEL. I didn't just pass him on the street!

AGNES. No, you didn't just meet him on a street——

RACHEL. Like your bookkeeper——

AGNES. You met him at Bickford's.

RACHEL [*defiantly*]. Longchamps! Honestly. I happen to be in love with him. That's why I'm wandering around this damn stupid—wondering—why the hell. Oh, Christ.

She sits back on the bed, stretches out, rolls over on her stomach, sobs once.

AGNES [*getting up*]. Oh, come on. Have a box of Kleenex.

RACHEL [*her face buried in the pillow*]. I don't want them.

AGNES. They pop up.

RACHEL. Go away. Why did I say anything? What had it cost me really? Nothing.

AGNES *goes to the desk, gets a bottle of liquor out of the bottom drawer, fixes two drinks—just liquor, no mix.*

AGNES. Honestly. Here. Have a shot. Me too, it's good for a cold. If I'm going to be running around nursing a roommate all night. Me? I'm always nursing someone else's broken heart. Just once I'd like a broken heart of my own.

RACHEL [*sitting up, takes the drink*]. You're great.

AGNES. I snore actually. Why don't you go to bed?

RACHEL. I can't. I don't think. You go on. . . . It isn't late, is it?

AGNES. No. I hate you like this, I pass up more good cracks.

RACHEL. I think maybe I should call in the morning.

AGNES. And tell them what? That he really didn't do it? Not here or in Denver or in Tucson? They knew twice what you did about him. [*Moving toward her purse on the vanity.*] I got a hangnail. Damn that typewriter.

RACHEL. I could drop the charges.

AGNES [*looking through her purse for a file*]. I doubt if they'd let him out for you. Besides, I don't know about you, but I'd be scared to death if he got out now.

RACHEL. I don't know what I should have done.

AGNES. Please don't worry about it. It's done. It's over; that's it.

RACHEL [*long sigh, not looking at* AGNES]. Yeah.

RACHEL *is sitting gloomily, looking off into space.*

AGNES [*finding something in her purse*]. You collect coins? [*Pause. No response.*] I got a Tasmanian penny at Riker's yesterday.

RACHEL [*not listening*]. No.

AGNES [*temptingly*]. It's got some crazy fruit tree on it.

RACHEL [*not listening*]. No.

AGNES [*two fingers in the air, making a hand shadow*]. See the rabbit? [*Pause.*] You going to bed soon? Why don't you read something?

RACHEL. I tried it.

AGNES. Turn on the radio.

RACHEL. I tried it.

AGNES. What haven't you tried?

RACHEL. Oh, I'm being such a lunk. Really. Who's your lunch with?

AGNES. The boss's son. Tonsils. I told you about him. [*Nasally.*] He talks like that. And with a Harvard accent yet. He's got the kind of face, I swear as soon as it gets warm he's going to put on a funny pair of sunglasses. [*Pause.*] I feel I should sympatize with you, but honestly, Rachel, I've seen this happen I'll bet ten times since I've been living with you.

RACHEL. Not exactly this.

AGNES. And you say, "not exactly this" every time. It's a bore; you know what I mean?

RACHEL. All right. It's a bore. I couldn't agree more. How many boy friends have I had? Since you've been here? Not so many.

AGNES. I'm not your datebook. I don't know.

RACHEL. Since you've known me?

AGNES. I don't know. What am I?

RACHEL. Roger. Just after you moved in.

AGNES. Floyd. You'd just broke up with.

RACHEL. Then Roger.

AGNES. Then Val.

RACHEL. Tom. Then Val.

AGNES. And Marvin. What a loser he was.

RACHEL. And Joe. Six. God. It's just too much.

AGNES. In what? Nine months. Not even a year.

RACHEL. They were nice guys, though. All of them, really.

AGNES. Oh, charmers. All. Burghers of Calais.

RACHEL. It's too much.

AGNES. It's an unearthly waste of time, you know? You know what you could do in nine months?

RACHEL. Very funny.

AGNES. I wasn't even *thinking* that! Jesus! I meant like get to know someone. Get married—get engaged, at least.

RACHEL. Well, with Joe it was nearly three months. [*Looks aside at the phone, then reaches for it and sets it in her lap.*] Oh, God.

AGNES [*at the vanity dresser, still filing her nails, she is not looking at* RACHEL. *She drops her file*]. Fuck! [*Bends to pick it up.*] I've got to quit saying that. Jesus. [*Looking at* RACHEL *now, who is very slowly dialing a number.*] Rachel. [*No response. Firmly, flatly.*] Rachel.

RACHEL [*not listening*]. What?

AGNES [*firmly, flatly*]. If you're calling your mother I'm moving out.

RACHEL [*not listening*]. What?

AGNES [*same inflection*]. I said if you're calling your mother I'm moving out. Out into the street, into the rain. I don't care; I'll be happier there. I'll catch pneumonia, I'll go to Saint Vincent's Hospital, I'll be happier there, believe me.

RACHEL [*putting the phone down*]. What's wrong?

AGNES. Nothing's wrong, I've just had it with the Daisy Mae routine.

RACHEL. It isn't that bad.

AGNES. You are on that phone for one minute and you have an accent strong enough to paper the walls. And I've lived with one Southern girl and couldn't take that, but this nightly metamorphosis bit I don't need.

RACHEL. Well, maybe it would help. There are times when you feel like calling your mother; what's wrong with that?

AGNES. Well, then; call my mother. But you get a line from here to Dogpatch, Virginia, and I'm moving out. I can't take it. I don't intend to sit here and listen to it. The days of the Cotton Queen are over as far as I'm concerned.

RACHEL. It isn't Dogpatch; I wish you'd quit saying that.

AGNES. What is it?

RACHEL. Cullerton.

AGNES [*flatly*]. Cullerton. Virginia.

RACHEL. North Carolina.

AGNES. North Carolina. Jesus. How long did it take you to learn to lose the drawl?

RACHEL. How long? About five years.

AGNES. Five years. To learn not to drawl. [*To herself.*] Van Gogh didn't study that long to learn. Of course he couldn't drawl. [*Winces, turns to the mirror.*] I'm going to put up my hair. I wasn't going to, but if we're up for the night.

RACHEL. Go on to bed. I think I will.

AGNES [*looks into the mirror*]. Oh, Jesus. [*Looks away blankly. Count ten. Looks back blankly. Count ten.*] Agnes, you're a vision. [*To RACHEL, without turning around. RACHEL slides under the covers of her bed, opens a magazine, doesn't read it.*] You know, three years ago I had kinky hair.

RACHEL [*without listening*]. No kidding.

AGNES. I had it straightened. [*Pause.*] Ever since I've had straight hair.

RACHEL. Why don't you just let it be straight; it looks nice like that.

AGNES. No. What I'm not is Veronica Lake. I used to go to this beautician—this gal. Nearly killed me. Inside. She says, Agnes—she was Jewish, you know—Agnes, she says, I'll do wonders for you—you won't recognize yourself. Your own mother won't know you. For nearly a year, every week. She'd comb me out and reset me exactly the same. Agnes, I'll do wonders for you. I came out looking exactly the same as I went in. Solid year.

RACHEL. Why did you keep going back to her then?

AGNES *begins to set her hair, rolling it onto large rollers and slipping a bobby pin onto the roller. This is a comically realistic process, done quite matter-of-factly.*

AGNES. I don't know. It's just nice to run into a positive attitude once in a while. I finally quit. She called me up after a couple of weeks, wanted to know what happened. I didn't have the heart to tell her my mother still recognized me. I told the beautician I'd bought a wig. [RACHEL *laughs.*] She tells me—oh, Agnes—you gotta bring it over. I do wonders with wigs. Your own mother won't recognize. . . . [*Pause.*] You gonna stay up all night or what?

RACHEL. I don't know. [*She stretches out in bed.*]

AGNES. Why did you ask for the bathroom if you don't want to shower or something, huh?

RACHEL. Look—Agnes—— [*Sitting up. Rather intense.*] Can we talk? Straight on this? So I can decide what I think for a minute, huh? Really, now—just straight for a minute or two and I'll be all right. I'll swear I don't know what the hell I'm going to do from here if I don't straighten myself out on this. I don't want to call Mom any more than you want me to, but I just want to——

AGNES [*getting up, she goes for a cigarette*]. Sure. Of course we can; talk to Doctor Muller. My fees are reasonable.

RACHEL. No, now—not even like that—just straight. So I know what I feel, or think or something! Sit down, now; stop flying around. See, I did like Joe and an awfully lot, too—

AGNES [*she has lit the cigarette. She sits down on the side of the bed opposite the table*]. Fine. Okay.

RACHEL. Well, don't interrupt! God.

AGNES. Okay, okay.

RACHEL. While you wrinkled up in that damn tub I honestly thought I was losing my mind; you come back in here and I say, Agnes: I think I'm losing my mind, could you take a minute out of your life to listen to me and I get twenty minutes of Charlie Chaplin.

AGNES. Okay! [*Pause.*] So go on.

RACHEL. I'm sorry. It's just, Jesus. I don't know anything; I just can't seem to do something that doesn't backfire, boomerang in my face. Blow up right in my face. I do something heatedly, because I'm mad and it's the right thing to do, I know—and then the whole thing blows up in my face. They're practically ready to hang Joe and all because I turned him in for filching some money from us. Not that much, really, either; I didn't talk to him, I just turned him in. God knows what kind of fix he was in to take money from us.

A rapid exchange follows between AGNES *and* RACHEL.

AGNES. You want a cigarette?

RACHEL. I just . . . NO! God! I don't want a cigarette.

AGNES. Okay, so you don't want a cigarette.

RACHEL. I just put one out. I have no urge for a cigarette at all. Thank you.

AGNES. I only asked, don't make a production out of it!

RACHEL. Well, I do not want a cigarette.

AGNES. Okay.

RACHEL. Is there anything else?

AGNES. All right, I said. *Christ!*

RACHEL [*intensely*]. Well I'm trying to say something and little Miss Helpful Agnes butts in with—

AGNES. Would you hand me the ash tray anyway?

RACHEL [*takes the ash tray, slams it down on the bed beside* AGNES. *Very loud. Jerky*]. CHRIST! Here! Cram it.

AGNES. I merely asked for the ash tray. [RACHEL *looks away, disgusted. Pause.*] Any particular place you'd like me to cram it? [*Silence.*] Well, I'm waiting for you to go on.

RACHEL [*still looking the other way. Quietly*]. Whenever you're ready.

AGNES. I'm ready.

RACHEL [*still not looking at* AGNES]. There's no point in my talking to myself. I could talk to myself by myself.

AGNES. I was listening to you.

RACHEL [*beginning to get tired, weary*]. Sure.

AGNES. I was. I heard every feeble-minded word you said.

RACHEL. Sure.

AGNES. You want me to repeat it?

RACHEL. No.

AGNES. You said, "God knows what kind of fix he was in to have to take money from us."

RACHEL [*silence. Then she turns to* AGNES]. Did I?

AGNES. You did. You said you do something and it blows up in your face; boomerangs, orangoutangs, backfires. And you do what's right and an innocent guy—which is a lie—is going to get hanged —which is a lie, and, "God knows what kind of fix he was in to have taken money from us." One more word and you'd have said, "It's only money."

RACHEL. Well, that's the stupidest thing I've ever said in my life then.

AGNES [*gets up*]. I'm going to roll my hair.

RACHEL. I can't even talk about him straight.

AGNES. What it boils down to is he was a damn good-looking stud and you——

RACHEL. Now, I resent that! For Christ's sake——

AGNES. Well, a good-looking guy then. And you're damn mad that you misjudged him and that you won't have him around again. And on top of that you trusted him enough to leave him here for a few hours when he was short—and you have to admit that he was very often short—and he took a month's pay from you. Now it's reasonable that you'd be pissed off. I would be too. I'd call the cops.

> *She turns to the mirror and continues to roll her hair.*

RACHEL. I did.

AGNES. Well, there you have it.

RACHEL [*sitting up in bed. Pause. Quietly; defensively*]. It isn't just physical.

AGNES [*not turning*]. When someone says it isn't just physical, you can be pretty sure it's just physical.

RACHEL [*sliding back down into bed*]. I guess I am tired. I didn't sleep at all last night. Are you going to bed?

AGNES. Not now. I probably couldn't breathe anyway. I need a respirator.

RACHEL. How come?

AGNES. All night long I've been telling you I was a dying woman. I have a cold.

RACHEL. Oh.

AGNES. In my head.

RACHEL [*sleepily, from beneath the covers*]. Why don't you rub yourself with Vicks or something?

AGNES. Because I've got a luncheon date with the boss's son and I don't want to smell like Vicks. Even for him. I'll give him my cold first.

RACHEL. That's silly.

AGNES [*quite to herself*]. His soup would probably taste like menthol, for Christ's sake.

RACHEL [*flopping over on her other side*]. I think I'm going to sleep.

AGNES [*paying no attention*]. "Suddenly it's springtime." [*Drops one of the rollers.*] Fuck. . . . I've got to quit saying that. [*Looks at the roller; gets up and picks it up; goes back to the vanity.*] Get some sleep.

RACHEL. It won't look so bad tomorrow—I know. You know, though; you're probably right. I just miss him a lot and in a few days I'll see everything in a better perspective.

AGNES. In a few days you'll be knocked up by some stud named Herkimer probably!

RACHEL [*sitting up*]. I will not be knocked up by anybody. . . . In a few days or nothing.

AGNES. Okay. I just meant, you've established a pattern by now. An orbit, so to speak, and by Thursday you'll be head-over-heels mad for someone totally different. You'll pass the sun again, so to speak.

RACHEL [*under the covers again*]. I'm not that bad.

AGNES. Very well, you're not that bad.

RACHEL. At least my mother would have told me it would be better tomorrow. That's all I need to get to sleep probably.

AGNES [*flatly*]. It'll be exactly the same tomorrow. "The world it was the old world yet. And I was I; my things were wet."

RACHEL [*half sits up again, disgusted*]. What?

AGNES. Nothing.

RACHEL. What do you mean, "My things were wet?"

AGNES. Nothing. It's a poem.

RACHEL. I know it's a——

AGNES. "Down in lovely muck I've lain; happy till I woke again. The world it was the old world yet and"——

RACHEL. ——"And I was I, my things were wet." So all right. What's lovely about a muck?

AGNES. He was drunk.

RACHEL. At Ludlow fair or some place, I know he was drunk. What's lovely about a muck?

AGNES. Well, maybe they pronounced it differently in Shropshire.

RACHEL. Very funny. [*Flopping back down.*] Are you coming to bed? I'm dead. I've just knocked myself out.

AGNES. Sure. You keep me awake all morning and ask me if I'm coming to bed.

RACHEL [*covered by the blankets*]. I'm sorry.

AGNES. Sure. You going to sleep or what?

RACHEL [*a little muffled*]. I said I was. If I can.

AGNES. Well sleep it off. I don't know why you should worry any more about Joe than you did about whoever it was before. You've got to admit the pattern is evident there somewhere. Maybe you should really go to an analyst, you know? No joke. You probably have some kind of problem there somewhere. [*She turns to her.* RACHEL *turns over.* AGNES *turns back to the mirror.*] I mean no one's normal. He's bound to find something. It might keep you away from dictionaries, you know? Jesus. [*Muffled noise from* RACHEL.] Well, I say if it helps, do it. To hell with how funny it looks. God knows I'd like to find—I'm absolutely getting pneumonia. [*Gets up to get the box of Kleenex and carries it back to the vanity, talking all the while.*] I'm going to be a mess tomorrow. I probably won't make it to work, let alone lunch. A casual lunch, my God. I wonder what he'd think—stupid Charles—if he knew I was putting up my hair for him; catching pneumonia. No lie, I can't wait till summer to see what kind of sunglasses he's going to pop into the office with. Probably those World's Fair charmers. A double unisphere. [*Turns.*] Are you going to sleep? [*Pause. No reply.*] Well, crap. [*Turning back to mirror.*] I may be tendering my notice, anyway. You've gone through six men while I sit around and turn to fungus. It's just not a positive atmosphere for me, honey. Not quite. You're out with handsome Val or someone and I'm wondering if the boss's skinny, bony son will come up to the water cooler if I. . . . [*Trails off, becomes interested in the roller. Now to someone—as at dinner.*] No. No Stroganoff. No, I'm on a diet. [*Correcting herself.*] No. I will not admit that. Good or bad if he says Stroganoff and baked potatoes it's Stroganoff and baked potatoes. And sour cream. And beer. He's probably on a diet himself. He could fill out, God knows. [*Turning to* RACHEL.] You know what Charles looks like? [*Pause.*] He looks like one of those little model men you make out of pipe cleaners when you're in grade school. [*Turning.*] Remember those? If I ever saw Charles without his clothes, he's so pale and white, I swear to God I'd laugh myself silly. He's Jewish, too. I'll bet his mother is a nervous wreck. I'll bet she thinks every woman on the block is pointing at her. Look, there goes Mrs. Schwartz; starving her children to death. Poor Charles. Shakes like a leaf. Of course Mrs. Schwartz wouldn't admit that either. No woman would admit her son was nervous; what's he got to be nervous about? The nerve of being nervous. My kid brother got an ulcer, my mother went to bed for three weeks, totally destroyed. Of course she spent about two thirds of her life totally destroyed. Upset—bawling. Weeks on end sometimes. My brother was great. He never paid the slightest attention to her; she'd get one of her spells and run off to bed bawling, it never bothered him for a minute. Off she'd go, the slightest provocation. Eric would say, "Mother's bedridden with the piss-offs again." I used to come home for a holiday or something and I'd say where's Mom and Eric would say, "Oh, she's bedridden with the piss-offs again." [*As if directly to someone, over lunch. Casually.*] You know, Charles, you've got nice eyes. You really have. Deep. I like brown eyes for a man. I don't like blue eyes, they always look weak or weepy. Either that or cold. You know? Brown eyes are warm; that's good. They're gentle. [*Quickly.*] Not weak, but gentle. [*Half to herself. Lightly.*] I used to want to have a girl; a little girl with blue eyes. For a girl that's good. So I used to always picture—God, idealize, really—very heavy-set, blond men. Swiss types, you know. [*Back to Charles.*] But a son I'd want to have brown eyes. That's better for boys. [*Looks at the sleeve of her robe.*] You think? [*Almost embarrassed.*] I don't know any more—— Oh, yes; I got it at Saks. It was on sale, I believe. [*Breaking off, disgusted.*] Now, what the hell does he care where I got it? And it wasn't on sale, knucklehead. And it wasn't Saks. [*Concentrating on her hair.*] It was Bonds. Not that he'd know the damn difference. [*She drops a roller, it bounces across the floor. She picks up another without even looking after the first one.*] Fuck. [*Finishing her hair.*] I've got to quit saying that.

This last said without listening to herself; second nature. She picks up a jar of cold cream, slowly, distantly, applies a dab to her lower lip. Pause. She sits still, staring off vacantly. A full thirty-second pause.

Curtain.

HOME FREE!

A Play in One Act

CHARACTERS

LAWRENCE BROWN
JOANNA BROWN
   Both are dark, attractive, about twenty-five or twenty-six.

SCENE: A small, cluttered room, where they eat and sleep. There may be a door to the kitchen, and there should be a front door. The room is several flights up. Important furnishings include a bed with a brightly colored quilt, a desk littered with paper, notebooks, etc. A candlelabrum, a music box, perhaps a dresser for JOANNA. There is a Ferris wheel which LAWRENCE has made; a large, colorful, highly decorated wheel which turns and has (perhaps ten or twelve) seats which swing as the wheel turns, all but two seats are on the wheel. A colorful box with a decorated lid, the Surprise Box, where gifts are placed. Perhaps a blackboard somewhere, and stools or chairs for Edna and Claypone, two imaginary characters who share the room. JOANNA is about six months pregnant.

This version of *Home Free!* was first presented by Joe Cino at the Caffe Cino, New York City, on August 23, 1964. It was directed by William Archibald with the following cast:

LAWRENCE	Michael Warren Powell
JOANNA	Maya Kenin

Sets and lighting by Mr. Archibald; assistant to the director was Charles A. Golden.

A subsequent production was staged by Theater 1965 at the Cherry Lane Theatre, New York City, on February 2, 1965, as part of their New Playwrights Series. It was directed by Marshall W. Mason with the following cast:

LAWRENCE	Michael Warren Powell
JOANNA	Joanna Miles

HOME FREE!

At rise we see LAWRENCE *in the room alone. He is tapping the wall with the end of a coat hanger to get the attention of his "audience": Claypone and Edna, his students for the moment.*

LAWRENCE. Now, if you'll only pay attention! The Pleiades are called the Seven Sisters because they're grouped closely together and with the unaided eye you can only see seven of them. Actually they're about thirty stars in the whole cluster. Now you know that the universe is expanding; we discussed that—Billy, sit down and don't chew your eraser—we discussed that last time. I know your name isn't Billy, Claypone, but you're pretending to be Billy: can't you just sit still like a good student? You're in Astronomy 101. If Edna can sit quietly, so can you. Now. As the universe is expanding and all of our galaxy is rotating, within the galaxy the stars are moving at incredible speeds in various directions. It's part of the expansion—Edna!—theory that all stars are moving farther and farther from each other. But the Seven Sisters, although they seem to be perfectly stationary to us, it has been proved that they are shooting away from the center— moving apart, at an incredible speed—every one getting farther from the others, so in a million years we won't be able to tell that they ever were a part of the same cluster. They're shooting out this way! [*Drawing, as with chalk, on the wall.*] And over here, and zoom—at about a hundred light-years a minute! Up and down and out and across—[*Getting uncontrollably excited, he starts tracing their path around the room as if following an exploded skyrocket.*]—and bang! And pow! And, if we was there, Whizz! Burn! Zing! Sssssstt Sssssstt! Zooommmmm! Kachowwie! Whamm! [*He has knocked some papers off the desk. He turns to Claypone, calming down.*] Hey, did I scare you? Did I? Where's Edna? [*His eyes focus under the desk across the room. Panting.*] You—come on back here, now. Come on. Sit down. You too, Claypone. It's part of the lesson. I'm busy now. You do something. I don't care; do anything. Don't bother me. [*He walks to the Ferris wheel, sitting, looking at it; turning it gently. To himself.*] No, no, if it went faster you wouldn't need the seats,

95

because the gravity would throw you against the bars; either that or it would throw you off altogether. Well, that way is all right, too; it's just that it's a different ride altogether. You'll have to experiment and see which principle applies to this particular size model. Well it might mean the death of a hundred-thirty-seven human guinea pigs, but if it's for the advancement of entertainment, what's a sacrifice? I am an engineer, a scientist, I can only make the models; you can either use them or disregard my advancements. [*To Claypone and Edna.*] No, she went to the grocery—she'll be back in a minute. No, you can't go out and look for her. They'd grab you and lock you in jail in a minute. Because you don't watch for street lights. You do not—every time—[*He is getting nervous, frightened.*]—you go out, you get almost hit with some car or truck and it just drives me crazy trying to keep track of you. And besides you hate it out there. You know how you are! You make me so ashamed—stuttering! And not talking to a person and wilting into some corner like a shade plant. No. She'll be back! She went to the grocery to get a few things! [*Almost uncontrolled.*] And she said she'll be back and she will. You must stay here. No, you stay too. You're not going to leave me here alone; you'd wilt into some corner and they'd come and take you off. [*He forces himself down between the desk and bed, on the floor.*] She'll be right back. She promised. And we'll look in the Surprise Box. She promised. You promised. She just went out for a minute; and she'll be back like always and tell us about the adventure, now. [*Pause. Music. Sweetly now.*] You just sit now, like you were at a social tea with ice cream and cake and peppermint frosting and little sugar cookies with butter and almond flavoring. And little sugar crystals on top that are red and blue and yellow and white. . . . [*There is a soft but very urgent knock at the door.*] Shhhhhhh! [*Violently whispered to Claypone and Edna.*] Be quiet! [*The knock is repeated a little louder.*] Shhh!

JOANNA [*from outside in a very urgent whisper*]. Quick, Lawrence. It's me. Quick; hurry. They're coming.

LAWRENCE [*hurries to the door, looks toward Claypone and Edna*]. It's okay, it's her. Sit down now and act like you've just been waiting nicely. Don't disappoint her. You just sit there. I'm coming.

JOANNA. Hurry.

LAWRENCE [to Claypone and Edna]. You be good. [He unlocks the door. JOANNA slips in and shuts it quickly. She stands just inside the door, her back to the wall. She locks the door quietly.]

JOANNA. Shhh! She saw me! [Still whispering.] She saw me coming in. She was right behind me. She's right outside. Shh! Listen!

LAWRENCE [as soon as she comes in he begins to whine. Over above]. Where have you been? They were just awful, they got so upset I hardly could control them.

JOANNA. Shhh!

Now LAWRENCE listens at the door too.

LAWRENCE [quickly to Claypone and Edna]. Don't say anything.

JOANNA. She was right behind me. I think she's outside the door. Listen.

LAWRENCE. Did she see you?

JOANNA. I don't think so. [Stops a moment; listens. In a normal voice, very casual.] No, it's okay, now.

LAWRENCE [still at the door]. Shhh! Listen!

JOANNA [a little winded]. No, it's okay now. Let me tell you!

LAWRENCE. I thought I heard something.

JOANNA. No, she's gone now. Sit down and I'll tell you about the adventure. [Still not able to catch her breath, she lays her hand against her pregnant belly.] Oh, poor old Tiberius and Coriolanus. They must wonder what I'm doing running upstairs. I'm sorry, Tiberius. I'm sorry, Coriolanus. My heart is just beating away.

LAWRENCE. Shhh! You aren't listening.

JOANNA. No. It's okay now. My heart is just pounding like crazy.

LAWRENCE [over, to Claypone and Edna]. You two!

JOANNA. Am I turning blue?

LAWRENCE [still whispering]. That isn't fair!

JOANNA. Feel how it's pounding. I shouldn't have run up those stairs but Pruneface was after me.

LAWRENCE. I'll feel the baby.

JOANNA [disgusted]. No. Claypone, sit down.

LAWRENCE. They were just awful while you were out. They were just terrible. I told Edna I was just gonna spank her good! If she didn't sit down and behave.

JOANNA [taking off her head scarf]. Well, she's young yet.

LAWRENCE. I said when my sister gets back here she's just gonna spank you good and proper.

JOANNA. Oh! [*Big announcement.*] He knows! Mr. Fishface knows. He asked about you. I've decided he knows the whole thing.

LAWRENCE. He asked after me?

JOANNA. Oh, he's getting so smarty, I'd like to just pinch him good. He said, "Where's your brother, Miss Brown?" And I said, "He isn't my brother, he's my husband; we're going to have a baby."

LAWRENCE. He said that?

JOANNA. Naturally I lied. He'll believe anything: I said, "He's my husband and he's in Bermuda just now and when he comes back he'll have a lovely dark tan." So you have to get a tan.

LAWRENCE. No.

JOANNA. Well, I'll think of something. Now. Sit down so I can tell you about the adventure.

LAWRENCE. Okay, Claypone sit there, she's going to tell us about the adventure. Edna, you stand there. And keep quiet!

JOANNA. Edna has to leave the room.

LAWRENCE. Edna, you must leave the room. Yes, you must! Through the kitchen and into the scullery and shut the door. And not a whimper out of you—

JOANNA [*in exactly the same voice*].—young miss! Go on this minute. [*She looks at Edna a moment.*] Well, I——!

LAWRENCE. What?

JOANNA. ——No, I wouldn't have said that. You can't say things that I wouldn't have said when I was a little girl. [*She has started out reprovingly but softens now.*] You might grow up to be different than me. You must wear tall black stockings and a long gray skirt and a wine-colored apron and your hair will be combed straight back and pulled into a bun and clipped with—— [*She makes a sudden, violent attack.*] Yes, it will, I did! [*Instantly sweet again.*] And clipped with a tortoise-shell bow. And you will sit with both your hands on your knees or folded in your lap and you will not think about what's between little boys' legs and you will speak when you're spoken to. [*She watches her go to the kitchen.*]

LAWRENCE. She's left.

JOANNA. She's listening. She has her ear against the door, she always does. [*Abruptly.*] Snoop! [*Listens.*] She's gone now. You know where she gets that—from that busybody landlady, Pruneface. [*She surveys Claypone and* LAWRENCE *and finds the situation satisfactory.*] Now. Actually, I only asked her to leave because I have an announcement to make. I will stand to—— [*As she starts to rise she catches her heart—lightly. Her voice now is surprised, serious.*] Oh, golly! [*Sits.*]

LAWRENCE [*over a bit*]. No, no, no announcements. You have to tell us about the adventure.

JOANNA. No, wait, golly—I shouldn't run. Well. This is——

LAWRENCE [*to Claypone*]. She's going to tell us about the adventure.

JOANNA. I will deliver my announcement from a seated position. Claypone, I want you to pay particular attention because you're involved.

LAWRENCE. I don't want to hear any old——

JOANNA. On my way outside to the grocery this afternoon, Miss Pruneface was in the hallway and she made me stop——

LAWRENCE [*over*]. What a silly thing to say—I don't know anybody by that name at all.

JOANNA [*without pause*]. And she said, "Mrs. Brown, I have told you before, you will have to move. You make too much noise as it is and"——

LAWRENCE [*over*]. She didn't say any such thing.

JOANNA. "And I'm afraid it will be impossible for you to live here after your baby is born."

LAWRENCE [*over a little*]. She did not.

Both speak at once.

JOANNA. "And I'm afraid it will be impossible for you to live here with an infant. You know I told you that when you moved in here." And I told you—and I told her we would—I did—you were not either—I was there. I told her we would be out next week!

LAWRENCE. She didn't even say one word to you. She didn't say anything. I went out. I was there. I went out after you did and she said we could stay here like we have been and we could stay on, she said as long as we wanted to!

JOANNA [*wins*]. So there!

LAWRENCE. No.

JOANNA. She looks at me in the hall and shakes her finger at me.

LAWRENCE. You told her a hundred times that we were moving and she never says anything more. You say that every week.

JOANNA. No. She looks at me and she says I can't have the baby here—because they don't want the noise, Lawrence.

LAWRENCE. It doesn't matter what they want.

There is a fast exchange between them.

JOANNA. They don't want the mess.

LAWRENCE. We just won't talk to her, then.

JOANNA. No, she'll throw us out in the street——!

LAWRENCE. We won't answer the door— Claypone, shut up!

JOANNA [*almost panicked*]. They're afraid of the baby, don't you know that?

LAWRENCE. ——Claypone's making noise!

JOANNA. They don't want the pain!

LAWRENCE. We won't go! We're not going. If you're not going to tell me about the adventure, I'm going to call Edna back into the room—Claypone go get Edna.

JOANNA. You sit right back down.

LAWRENCE. Well, then, we're going to look in the Surprise Box— it's wonderful.

JOANNA. No. No, you can't until two o'clock today.

LAWRENCE. No, come on—it's especially lovely, I bet, today.

JOANNA. Not until after I tell you about the adventure. I have not told you.

LAWRENCE. Very well—first she's going to tell us about the adventure.

JOANNA. To begin—there was a shadow across the door downstairs.

LAWRENCE. The sun is shining.

JOANNA [*she notices the interruption but goes on*]. It was all crooked because of the panels in the door, as usual; exactly the same number of squares in the sidewalk from here to the corner.

LAWRENCE [*quickly*]. Eighteen.

JOANNA. And—[*Pause. Sharply.*] I guess you just don't want to hear about it, do you?

LAWRENCE [*meaning "What did I do?"*]. What?

JOANNA [*continuing to look sharply at him*]. The same number of parking meters from here to the corner. [LAWRENCE *starts to speak up automatically; her look intensifies; he stops without really knowing why. When she is satisfied he is not going to interrupt she continues.*] Out of which eight were expired this morning. If you must know, I was thinking about the Ferris wheel most of the time I was out.

LAWRENCE. Do you want to look in the Surprise Box?

JOANNA. I don't think so; not till it's time. Unless you want to. It wasn't much of an adventure except for Mr. Fishface at the

market. The Skinner was watching me so I couldn't slip any-
thing. I think he's catching on. Old Fishface, though, he said:
"Oh, how's your brother, Miss Brown?" I said, "It's Mrs. Brown,
and he's not my brother as you are mistakenly referring to the
gentleman whose company you've seen me in. That's Mr. Brown,
and he's away in the Canary Islands trapping finches but we're
expecting him shortly, Mr. Fishface. I'll give him your best."
LAWRENCE. Lie.
JOANNA. I said that. I did.
LAWRENCE. You didn't say, "Mr. Fishface."
JOANNA. I most certainly did.
LAWRENCE. Claypone, she didn't. [*They are beginning to laugh.*]
JOANNA. I did. And I said, "How's Mrs. Fishface?"
LAWRENCE [*laughing*]. You did not.
JOANNA [*laughing*]. And all the little tadpoles that must be swim-
ming around at home. And all——
LAWRENCE. —And the pollywogs! And—
*They degenerate into a giggling mess, falling all over each other
and slapping at each other. They fall onto the bed, giggling.*
JOANNA. And the little baby perch.
LAWRENCE. And the whole Fishface family.
They try to stop laughing. JOANNA *tries to sit up on the bed.*
JOANNA. Come on. Be serious.
LAWRENCE [*pulling her back down*]. No.
JOANNA [*sitting up again*]. Yes— Go away, Claypone—sit down.
[*To* LAWRENCE.] I don't know why we keep him around, he's so
stupid. [*As he tries to pull her back down.*] Oh, don't—I get dizzy
today. You know I can't play much at a time.
LAWRENCE. Oh, you're always dizzy. Now let's look in the Surprise
Box.
JOANNA. No, wait! I forgot the most important part! A cat! [*This is
used to draw his attention away from the Surprise Box as she slips
a fountain pen into it a bit later.*] A yellow and gray and white
and brown and——
LAWRENCE. Not brown. Lie!
JOANNA. Brown! With black ears—all spots—ran across from the
market and under a parked car. I called to her but she wouldn't
come. She only looked out from behind a tire and wouldn't come.
LAWRENCE. How did you know it was a she-cat?

JOANNA. Because she was fat and pregnant like me! No tomcat is going to have kittens.

LAWRENCE. Maybe you'll have kittens though! Spotted kittens!

JOANNA. Oh! Wouldn't that be *rare*? Why how rare! But I know I won't. I just couldn't. Nothing ever happens like that. Seldom ever.

LAWRENCE. Or pups! You never know what can happen. [JOANNA *slips the pen into the box.*] Now let's look in the Surprise Box. [*The lid bumps softly.*] Did you peek? You peeked!

JOANNA. Lie! I never did. [*To Claypone.*] Tell him! Now see?

LAWRENCE. Okay. Let's look now.

> *They walk to either side of the box.*

JOANNA. Okay.

> *They both close their eyes.*

LAWRENCE. Open it.

> *She does.*

JOANNA. It's open.

> *They open their eyes.*

LAWRENCE. A pen! Where did you find it?

JOANNA. I have no idea where it came from. Maybe you can use it to write your book. [*Looking into the box with wonder.*] Ohh! I'll bet *someone* has sure been busy. Another seat for the Ferris wheel. [*She lifts it out gently.*] Oh, it's lovely. It's so lovely. This is the best one so far—it's so *fragile*!

LAWRENCE. It's not too fragile, though, I don't think.

JOANNA. Oh, no. It just looks——

LAWRENCE. Where do you suppose it came from?

JOANNA. I'll bet I know. I'll bet Lawrence Brown made it while I was out.

LAWRENCE. Do you suppose. . . .

JOANNA. I certainly do suppose. Can I put it on? You can come over, Claypone, and watch.

LAWRENCE [*nods*]. Carefully.

JOANNA. Well, I won't break it. It's my surprise, after all. [*She sets it gently on the Ferris wheel.*] There. Is that all? Count them, Claypone.

LAWRENCE. One more to go yet.

JOANNA. Then it'll be totally finished.

LAWRENCE. I'll bet no one has anything at all like this Ferris wheel.

JOANNA. After you get just one more seat done——

LAWRENCE. And then we can get in it and riiide like mad. [JOANNA *is turning it very slowly.*] Easy! [*Said softly to* JOANNA, *but as she starts to frown at him he adds quickly.*] Claypone, easy!

JOANNA *automatically switches her frown to Claypone and they both frown briefly at him.*

JOANNA. Clutz. [*To* LAWRENCE.] Why we have to harbor a forty-three-year-old imbecile!

LAWRENCE [*as the Ferris wheel turns*]. Up we go.

JOANNA. I don't think it's for us to ride. I think it's for the baby.

LAWRENCE. Well, maybe all three—or you two and I'll turn.

JOANNA. It's lovely. The last seat is the best, *I* think, anyway. Technically.

LAWRENCE. I can make this pen work. It's 14 carat gold.

JOANNA. Where?

LAWRENCE. There. And Parker. There.

JOANNA. You can use it to write your book with.

LAWRENCE. Hey, wonderful.

JOANNA. What do you think we should call it, Lawrence?

LAWRENCE. We? I get to name my book by my——

JOANNA. No, no, no. Not your old book. You're so stupid.

LAWRENCE. Lie!

JOANNA. Claypone, isn't he stupid?

LAWRENCE. Lie!

JOANNA. Lie! Lawrence, you're stupid. My *baby*. What will we name it?

LAWRENCE. *Our* baby.

JOANNA. Our baby. What will we call it?

LAWRENCE. I thought we settled on something yesterday. Boy or girl?

JOANNA. I think girl.

LAWRENCE. We'll name her—Miss Brown.

JOANNA [*starting to say no*]. Well, why not? Perfect!

LAWRENCE. The name will be perfect but I don't suppose we can expect the baby to be. I don't see how Miss Brown can help being deformed a little.

JOANNA. Mmmm. Maybe no arms.

LAWRENCE. Very well: no arms. At least she won't go around breaking things. You should concentrate on no voice box too.

JOANNA. I don't think that's nice. You hate children. What kind of father is that? You have no business being a father at all if you hate children.

LAWRENCE. I don't hate them. I hate the noise they make.

JOANNA. Claypone, what can you do with a father who hates children?

LAWRENCE. Well, what's so unusual about that? Besides, I don't hate them all. I think I begin to like them as soon as they're about fifteen years old.

JOANNA. What do I do with her till then?

LAWRENCE. I don't know. Send her to camp!

JOANNA [delighted at the idea]. Of course. Send her to camp! Lackawalla Nursery, then Lackabellabella Camp and Miss Lackamannamanna's Home for Young Ladies.

LAWRENCE. And we'll be home riding the Ferris wheel. She's going to be no problem. [Puts his head to JOANNA's stomach.] Are you going to be a problem, Miss Brown? What was that? You're all muffled. She says no.

JOANNA. Well, she's different.

LAWRENCE. That's right, I'd forgotten.

JOANNA [calling]. You can come back now, Edna. Here, quick; kiss me. [They kiss; she looks up as Edna enters.] Oh, you weren't supposed to see that.

LAWRENCE. We were discussing things you're not old enough to understand, young lady. When you grow up maybe we'll tell you.

JOANNA. And maybe we won't.

LAWRENCE. Now let's go. I want to go off to bed. Come on.

JOANNA. No. Not now.

LAWRENCE. What kind of wife are you? It's part of the common law—you have to come when I tell you to.

JOANNA. I'm not your wife, I'm your sister.

LAWRENCE. Well, what kind of sister are you?

JOANNA. Only if I'm in agreement, and I don't fancy it. I want to at two o'clock. And nothing will——

LAWRENCE. Shhhh! Listen! I thought I heard something. That's twenty minutes. We can start now.

JOANNA. No, we won't start now. That isn't fair. There's no point in having a schedule if you don't stick to it religiously.

LAWRENCE. That's absurd.

JOANNA. Not at all. I have a very simple timetable here I've worked out. I'm quite mathematical, you know.

LAWRENCE. You are not mathematical at all. But I'll wait till two o'clock. And we can take Colonel Polarfuz with us. No, Edna, you slept with him last night. Wipe your nose!

JOANNA. Colonel Polarfuz was with us when I got pregnant. Every time you take the teddy bear I get pregnant.

LAWRENCE. That isn't true. He's been with us a hundred times and you haven't got pregnant but once.

JOANNA. Well, I will again. On top of Miss Brown. Or maybe Miss Brown will get pregnant. I'll have one and in three months I'll have another and the first thing you know I'll be turning them out like Volkswagens. Besides, when I have Miss Brown we have to move away.

LAWRENCE. No, Joanna. You can't have it if we have to move away.

JOANNA. Yes. Are we going to be good parents?

LAWRENCE. No.

JOANNA. Yes, we are.

LAWRENCE. Okay. The perfect parents. We can even get married.

JOANNA. But we have to move. The city isn't any place to prepare a child anyway. She can't grow up in the city——

LAWRENCE. ——Ha! Prepare——

JOANNA. ——What's funny? What's funny, Edna?

LAWRENCE. You said "prepare." [*To Edna.*] She said "prepare." The city is no place to prepare a child——

JOANNA. Well, it isn't.

LAWRENCE [*pretending to be a chef*]. To prepare one City Child, stew softly in mother's milk for two hours or until tender——

JOANNA [*joining in*]. ——Turning frequently. City Children are poached in milk.

LAWRENCE. And in the country——

JOANNA. The Country Child is simmered in butter——

LAWRENCE. ——And onions! [*Takes up a paper and pencil.*]

JOANNA. Chop twelve large red onions very fine——

LAWRENCE. That's too fast, let me write it down.

JOANNA. Chop twelve large Bermuda onions—we'll send it to *Good Housekeeping*. "Dear Cooking Editor. This recipe has been in our family for nine centuries"——

LAWRENCE. Generations. For nine generations.

JOANNA. ——Grease lightly one Dutch oven.

LAWRENCE. And there has to be vegetables——

JOANNA [*quitting the game abruptly*]. We have to move anyway. Lady Pruneface looks at me every time I pass her in the hall or on the stairs. She looks at my bulging middle.

LAWRENCE. Well, if you'd learn to hold your stomach in like I told you.

JOANNA. She's thinking when Miss Brown comes out—we go out.

LAWRENCE. Maybe it won't be Miss Brown—maybe it'll be kittens. With kittens she'd look the other way.

JOANNA. I saw a cat!

LAWRENCE. You told us. Honestly, sometimes you don't have all your marbles.

JOANNA. I didn't tell you, Edna. Besides I saw another one: a dead one.

LAWRENCE. Why didn't you get it? You should have brought it home free.

JOANNA. It was too dead.

LAWRENCE. What color?

JOANNA. I couldn't tell.

LAWRENCE. Gray then. Maybe it won't be kittens. Maybe it'll be pups. Pups she'd look the other way.

JOANNA. Not a chance. It's too rare. It seldom ever happens any more. You know that.

LAWRENCE. It's almost two o'clock. I can't wait.

JOANNA. You've got to. Sit down and wait. I don't mind going back on my word in front of Claypone, but not Edna. We should be an example to her. Why don't you work on your book?

LAWRENCE. I decided to illustrate it myself.

JOANNA. I didn't realize you were talented.

LAWRENCE. I'm not, silly—but it's going to be very, very modern. [*To Edna.*] No, you can't! In color. [*He gets pencil and paper at his desk and sits.*] It'll be about Miss Brown and getting lost in the woods.

JOANNA. And you must describe the woods in every possible detail. Every leaf and every bird.

LAWRENCE. Very well. Don't bother me then, I'm going to write until two o'clock and then we'll go to bed. Now sit down. You too, Edna. And Claypone. Sit there. Now! And don't say a word.

Pause while he thinks. JOANNA *sits.*

JOANNA. Don't chew your pencil.

LAWRENCE. Shhhh!

JOANNA. Well, I'm not sitting here and watching you devour a perfectly good pencil. Chew a cigar or something if you want to chew.

LAWRENCE. Shhhhh!

JOANNA [*pause. Helpfully*]. Would you care for |a stick of gum?

LAWRENCE. No thank you, Joanna. Just sit there and be still. [*Without looking up.*] Edna, stop fidgeting. [*Pause. He thinks and writes a few words.* JOANNA *becomes restless. Gets up and wanders to the Surprise Box. She winds the music box, he reacts. She stops. Then opens music box for one note. He snorts. She closes it, turns around, and studies him.*]

JOANNA. A boy looked at me on the subway last night. [*Pause. No reaction.*] He said "hello"!

LAWRENCE. When? [*Pause. No reaction.*] When?

JOANNA. I didn't say anything, I looked the other way. Last night.

LAWRENCE. What'd he say?

JOANNA. He said hello and I turned my hand so he could see I was married and I looked the other way.

LAWRENCE. Lie. You went away with him.

JOANNA. Lie, I looked the other way. [*To Edna.*] I did too, young lady, you just shut your mouth or I'll wash it out with soap! [*To* LAWRENCE.] I looked the other way and he got off the train. Now go on writing.

LAWRENCE. What'd he look like?

JOANNA. I didn't notice.

LAWRENCE. What'd he *look* like?

JOANNA. I didn't notice, now go on writing. [*Beat.*] He had blond curly haid and a very square jaw and a sweater with a big red "R" on it. [*Quickly to Edna.*] I did not, young lady, you shut up!

LAWRENCE. Some college boy, they'll flirt with married women, it makes them feel big.

JOANNA. Well, I looked the other way and he got off the train. Aren't you going to write?

LAWRENCE. I can't do anything if you're going to talk all the time. You're just jealous because you don't have anything to do. I'll do something else.

JOANNA. Lie! I certainly am not.

LAWRENCE. Well, I'll do something else anyway. Let's go to bed.

JOANNA. Shhhh! [*Listens.*] Not now.

LAWRENCE. What? I'll move the clock up.

JOANNA. That isn't fair. You're a cheat.

LAWRENCE. You are. Edna, leave the room!

JOANNA. I said I wouldn't. [*To Edna.*] You sit right back down, young miss. You just do what I do. [*To* LAWRENCE.] Edna and Claypone can read. [*To them.*] You can read. I don't care—anything. [*To* LAWRENCE.] And you and I will talk about moving.

LAWRENCE. I won't talk about any such thing!

JOANNA. We have to talk about it. We have to. She's right behind the door and besides Miss Brown will probably be blue!

LAWRENCE. Not blue. Shut up about blue.

JOANNA. If I was a blue baby she'll be a blue baby. It's simple heredity.

LAWRENCE. You were not a blue baby. You just make it up so you'll sound exceptional.

JOANNA. Mother said I was a blue baby and they sewed me back up and I am too exceptional.

LAWRENCE. What does she know about it?

JOANNA. . . . Besides I can feel the catgut.

LAWRENCE. I don't want to hear about your pains and catgut. Honestly, sometimes you can really be nauseating . . . [*Mumbling.*] Catgut.

JOANNA. I had another one.

LAWRENCE. I don't want to hear about it.

JOANNA [*holding her shoulder*]. I felt it here. Feel.

LAWRENCE. That shows what you know about it. Heart pains are felt in the bottom of the stomach.

JOANNA. Well, mine hurts me here. You know it does. You were scared once.

LAWRENCE. When was I? I was not. You were faking and I knew it.

JOANNA. Lawrence Brown, you were so.

LAWRENCE. Joanna Brown, I was not. I wasn't. You made it up; you did.

JOANNA. I didn't.

LAWRENCE. I wasn't. You never had one of your pains!

JOANNA. I feel it all the time.

LAWRENCE. I won't listen to you. I have to write.

JOANNA [*louder*]. I feel it in my shoulder like someone pinching me!

LAWRENCE [*louder*]. I won't listen to you. I'll sing!

JOANNA [*louder*]. I DO! I can feel it right now!

LAWRENCE [*singing loudly*]. My country tis of thee—sweet land of liberty! Of thee I sing! Land where!——

JOANNA. Okay! They are trying to read. You can at least be civil. I know it's difficult for you, but if you will only try.

LAWRENCE. You started it by faking.

JOANNA. Well, I feel it!

LAWRENCE [*sings two notes very loudly*]. Land where!——

JOANNA. But I won't talk about it. Shhh! Listen.

LAWRENCE. What?

JOANNA. Shhh! She's gone. You won't learn, will you?

LAWRENCE. Well, you started it by faking . . . you think you're so very exceptional.

JOANNA. Well, I *am exceptional!*

LAWRENCE. You are not! You're blue and that's not exceptional.

JOANNA. *You* shut up!

LAWRENCE. Turn blue for me. Just once!

JOANNA. I. Will. Not!

LAWRENCE. You can't.

JOANNA. I could if I wanted to. I wouldn't be inclined to for you.

LAWRENCE [*pause*]. Are we really going to be turned out? Did she honestly say no children?

JOANNA. She only told us a dozen times.

LAWRENCE. Well, what does she expect a young married couple to do?

JOANNA. We're not married.

LAWRENCE. Well we told her we were. We'll get a lawyer.

JOANNA. We can't. He'd guess. You know how lawyers are. They'd even take away Miss Brown. [*To Edna.*] They can *have* you!

LAWRENCE. He'd guess from your eyes.

JOANNA. Certainly not! You'd tell him. You'd stammer and stutter and he'd know. You always stutter when you talk to anyone but me!

LAWRENCE. I do not!

JOANNA. You stutter and stammer and just wilt into a corner like some shade plant.

LAWRENCE. Stop.

JOANNA. You just can't—[*Whining.*]—cross the street—— Oh, I can't *talk* to anyone. Oh, that truck is going to hit me!

LAWRENCE. Don't.

JOANNA [*calmer*]. You always embarrass me when you talk to the landlady.

LAWRENCE. Well, I can't talk to Pruneface. She's wrinkled. She has white hair, that's the reason. [JOANNA *smiles and doesn't speak.*] It is, too!

JOANNA. I didn't say a word. I agree with you. I really do. [*Pause.*] Mr. Fishface doesn't have white hair and you stutter to him!

LAWRENCE. He's got a fish——

JOANNA. I didn't hear you.

LAWRENCE. He's got——

JOANNA. I didn't say a word.

LAWRENCE. I have to write. Why don't we go to bed and play?

JOANNA. I'm not in the mood. You'd stutter.

LAWRENCE. Lie! That *was* a lie! Tell her, Claypone.

JOANNA. You're just a mess.

LAWRENCE. You are! You live in common law!

JOANNA. So do you.

LAWRENCE. So do you!

JOANNA. It's different with me. I'm a girl. [*To Edna.*] We girls are very exceptional.

LAWRENCE. You live in common law.

JOANNA. I was a blue baby! And besides, I have a pain.

LAWRENCE. I'll give you a pain. You always have a pain when you're in the wrong. I'll kiss it and make it well.

JOANNA. Go away. It feels like pinching. Really.

LAWRENCE. You're faking. You want attention because you're pregnant.

JOANNA. That's a perfectly acceptable reason. Ask any woman—until the child is born any woman is a very very special and wonderous thing. [*Regally.*] As a matter of fact, I'm royalty. I'm a queen! [*Simply.*] I have blue blood.

LAWRENCE. A queen! [*Music for two or three bars, very faint.*] A queen! I should have recognized it. Queens are always pregnant with somebody or other. Prince Claypone! Fetch her the crown. Lady Edna, Lady Edna—into the kitchen and supervise those wenches. Into the kitchen with you!

JOANNA [*assuming the air of a gruff queen*]. Bring me a pickled flamingo, Lady Edna!

LAWRENCE [*bringing a chair*]. Sit here on this throne. Up with your feet on the ottoman.

JOANNA [*kicking aside the chair*]. Down with the Ottomans! Behead every one of them. Barbarians! I won't have them in the kingdom! Where's my filet of flamingo? Behead that girl!

LAWRENCE [*with a quilt from the bed*]. You must have a mantle. This robe, your pregnancy, was made by four hundred Hungarian virgins who went blind sewing seed pearls. [*Getting a candelabrum.*] And a scepter! Is there anything else, your pregnancy?

He tucks in the quilt.

JOANNA [*gruffly*]. Careful with me, you fool. I'm with child! You're *jostling* the future king!

LAWRENCE [*excited. Again singing. Loud*]. For unto us a child is given. For unto us a son is born. And the government shall be upon his shoulders! And his name shall be——

JOANNA. Silence! Silence that racket or off with your shoulders!

LAWRENCE. Oh, no. Not that. Not that, your pregnancy. Not my shoulders! Throw me in the briar patch, but not my shoulders!

JOANNA [*saintly*]. I knight. Thee. [*Pause.*] Sir Stutter! Ha!

LAWRENCE. That's not fair! You're a whore. [*Takes away quilt.*] You're not a queen. Fetch your own filet of flamingos. Edna— forget the flamingos. She's not a queen, she's a whore.

JOANNA. Oh! I *am not!*

LAWRENCE. I bet you are!

JOANNA. I bet I am not!

LAWRENCE. I bet you go around trying to stir up some look in boys' eyes.

JOANNA. I bet I do not.

LAWRENCE. Lie!

JOANNA. Lie! I do not. Only you. You know it's true. I couldn't get away if I wanted to. Besides, now I'm pregnant.

LAWRENCE. I'd hold you in. [*Moving behind her.*] I'd bite the nape of your neck and pull you back like a tomcat.

JOANNA [*playfully*]. Ouch! It tickles.

LAWRENCE. Of course it tickles. Let's take a shower.

JOANNA. No. Oh, sometimes you're really vulgar. Sometimes you really shock us.

LAWRENCE. Shock you. I do not.

JOANNA. You do, too. You do.

LAWRENCE. Let me feel the baby. [*Reaches around her. To Edna.*] Do you want to feel the baby?

JOANNA [*to Edna*]. No! No, you can't. You'd hit. I know you.

LAWRENCE. I think she's asleep. [JOANNA *touches her shoulder*.]

JOANNA. Ouch, Lawrence!

LAWRENCE. I'm not hurting. You don't suppose she's asleep. Hey, wake up, Miss Brown. God, you don't suppose she's going to be lazy, do you? Edna, you knock over that Ferris wheel and I'll hit you good!

JOANNA. Of course she's not going to be lazy.

LAWRENCE. If there's anything I can't tolerate it's laziness. Why doesn't she kick or something?

JOANNA. I like it when she takes these little cat naps——

LAWRENCE. Do you suppose she'll really be a whole litter of kittens?

JOANNA. ——Lord knows she kicks me enough when she's awake. [*To Edna*.] She's going to take after you, you little sadist. [*Touches her shoulder*.] Oh, golly.

LAWRENCE. What's wrong?

JOANNA. I had a little pain is all.

LAWRENCE. Miss Brown kicked you!

JOANNA. In the shoulder. You don't seem to realize that Mrs. Pruneface is just outside that door and she's going to kick us out onto the street and I have a pain.

LAWRENCE. Oh, that! [*To Edna*.] Don't believe her.

JOANNA. You never believe anything I say. None of you. Well, you'll see.

LAWRENCE. Hey. Come to bed with me now.

JOANNA. I will, I guess. If you'll only be quiet. It's nearly time.

LAWRENCE [*singing*]. It's nearly time, it's nearly time.

JOANNA. And if you'll promise to talk about moving away afterwards.

LAWRENCE. Afterwards they lay on the soft grass and talked about moving away.

JOANNA [*happy*]. I wish I wasn't pinching.

LAWRENCE. I'll teach you to pinch.

JOANNA. The whole world pinches me!

LAWRENCE [*singing*]. He's got the whole world—between his finger and thumb.

JOANNA. You always sing when I say we'll go to bed!

LAWRENCE. It makes me happy. I like it.

JOANNA. That's all you know. Hop in bed. You're a funny rabbit.

LAWRENCE. I'm a funny rabbit. [*To Edna*.] Are you a funny rabbit?

JOANNA. Impossible rabbit. I love an impossible rabbit. Oh, God!
LAWRENCE. What?
JOANNA. Well, think of all the number of offspring rabbits have.
LAWRENCE. Wonderful.
JOANNA. That's all perfectly well for the buck—but I have to bear all those scratchy little monsters. Fuzzy little monsters.
LAWRENCE. You'll die laughing! It sounds like fun.
JOANNA. Everything sounds like fun to you.
LAWRENCE. Everything is.
JOANNA. How do you suppose a female rabbit keeps from giggling? I mean, think how furry a baby rabbit is.
LAWRENCE. They really are, you know. [*To Edna.*] Of course they are, Edna. And long tickly ears. But giggling isn't bad.
JOANNA. Well, maybe not—but it certainly would destroy the seriousness of the situation.
LAWRENCE. You giggle better than any rabbit anyway.
JOANNA. Oh, I never giggle. [*Picks up music box.*]
LAWRENCE. Oh, you don't?
JOANNA. What?
LAWRENCE. You never giggle. You don't, huh?

He starts advancing slowly toward her.

JOANNA. No-o-o-a.
LAWRENCE. You don't giggle ever, huh?
JOANNA. Now you stay away. I can't play like that.

She is smiling.

LAWRENCE. Not even with someone playing the piano on your ribs? Get back, Claypone.
JOANNA [*touching her shoulder*]. You stay away now. I don't giggle.

They are laughing now.

LAWRENCE. Edna? Did you hear what she said? She said she doesn't snicker. Not even a little. Whatta you think of that?
JOANNA. Now that isn't true. [*They are circling the room.*] I didn't say I don't snicker. I said I don't giggle. I snicker all the time.
LAWRENCE. You giggle too. Admit it.
JOANNA. I snicker like a horse. It's *disgusting* the way I snicker. [*She half throws, half lays the music box on a chair.*] Move back, now Edna, don't you help him.

There is a full-scale chase.

LAWRENCE. You're going to giggle.

He knocks the chair over.

JOANNA. Stay back, I said!

From the floor the music box plays.

LAWRENCE. No. We're going to make you giggle.

JOANNA. No, you aren't.

LAWRENCE. I am. Claypone, head her off.

JOANNA. Don't do it, Claypone. I'll tell Mother on you.

LAWRENCE. Mother's in heaven and Mother can't hear you.

JOANNA. Mother's in Hoboken and if I yell loud enough she'll *hear me*. The whole *building* will hear me!

LAWRENCE. They'll hear you giggle when I catch you.

JOANNA. They won't!

She pulls out a chair and runs behind the table. Sudden stop. Scream. JOANNA's *expression is one of terror and great pain.* LAWRENCE *is still playing. He thinks she is joking.*

LAWRENCE. Everyone will hear you laugh your——

JOANNA. Get away.

She can't speak further.

LAWRENCE. What's wrong? [*She turns to him.*] Oh, come on! That's not fair. That isn't fair. Edna, don't believe her, she's joking. She's pretending.

JOANNA [*starting to collapse*]. It's pinching me . . .

LAWRENCE. I don't believe you.

Still he takes her and starts to help her to the bed.

JOANNA. Oh, really, Lawrence, really!

LAWRENCE. I don't believe you. That's foolishness. I'm not going to get frightened again, if that's what you're trying.

JOANNA. Am I blue?

LAWRENCE. Really? You truly hurt? [*He is getting scared and excited.*] I'll help you, don't worry. I'll get you something. What do you want, Joanna?

JOANNA. A doctor. Oh, please.

LAWRENCE. A doctor? They know everything. I'll get you a doctor. [*But he stays by the bed.*] I will.

JOANNA. Lawrence, go. Go on, hurry.

LAWRENCE. I will. I'll get you anything, Joanna. [*Panicked.*] Tell me what you want, rabbit.

JOANNA. Downstairs and on the corner—get me a doctor.

LAWRENCE. No, now I can't go out there, Joanna, you know I don't go out there, you said I——

JOANNA. Please, Lawrence——

LAWRENCE. ——*never had* to go out there—now, I can't do something——

JOANNA [*screams, but the wind cuts away from her voice*]. No. Go on, Lawrence. Look, it's okay. It's okay. There's nothing out there that will hurt you, it's——

> LAWRENCE *has gone to the door.*

LAWRENCE. No, she's out there—she's right on the other side of the door. I can't go out there.

JOANNA. Lawrence, it's never been like this. Go on!

LAWRENCE. [*crumpling at the door*]. No, I can't. I can't. Don't make me. Don't make me. Please don't make me. I can't go out—— They'll take me off—— I can't go, don't make me, Joanna, please don't.

JOANNA [*over the above, coaxingly*]. Lawrence, look, baby, it's okay, baby, there's nobody out there who can hurt you, baby, Lawrence, for Me. Please. Please.

> Her strength fails.

LAWRENCE. Joanna? Say things to me, Joanna. [*She looks at him.*] Joanna?

JOANNA. Please. [*She takes a jar and knocks it violently against the wall, calling.*] Miss Williams! Miss Williams!

LAWRENCE. NO! Don't call old Pruneface! I'll get you a doctor, I really will, Joanna. It's okay. Quick, quick, EDNA! Put on your coat, child, this is an emergency. [*He runs and opens the door just enough for Edna to squeeze through.*] As fast as you can or she'll die. There's a doctor's sign over the drugstore on the corner.

JOANNA. No, Lawrence! You go. You go. YOU GO!

LAWRENCE [*turning to her*]. It's all right. She went for him. You have to be patient. Can I get you something? You'd feel better if you sat up and talked, I'll bet. [*She has tried to sit up. She falls back.*] Here, I'll sit by you and hold your hand. [*He takes her hand; it falls lifeless and unnoticed from his.*] Now, don't go to sleep, she'll be right back in no time. I told her to hurry. It's after two o'clock already. I wish you'd sit up and—I know what—I want to show you something. [*He gets a seat for the Ferris wheel*

from the table where he'd hidden it.] If there's something in the
Surprise Box. [*He puts it in but is too excited to leave it there.*]
Joanna, I bet there's something in the Surprise Box. [*He opens
it.*] I wonder . . . Look. [*He brings it over to her.*] See? I made
two of them and this one is. . . . If I put it on the Ferris wheel,
will you sit up? If—I tell you—you can put the last one on. . . .
If I—what if I—look. [*He sets it on the wheel.*] Joanna? Look at
that! It's all finished, Joanna. Are you going to sleep? It's all
finished—you're supposed to be the very first one to turn it.
. . . Look, if I let you. . . . If I turned it for you then you—
would you—then would you? Huh? Look, what . . . if I see? [*He
turns it slowly around.*] See? Well, If I If I If I If I took—If I
went—let you take—if I got, then, would. . . . If I then would
. . . you . . . would. . . you. . . .

Curtain.

About the Author

Born in Lebanon, Missouri, in 1937, Lanford Wilson grew up in Ozark, Missouri. He attended college in San Diego and Chicago. *Home Free!* was written in 1963 and revised in April 1964. *Balm in Gilead* was completed in July 1964 and *Ludlow Fair* in October of the same year.

Mr. Wilson is a founding member of the Circle Repertory Company in New York and one of twenty-one resident playwrights for the company. His work at Circle Rep includes *The Hot l Baltimore* (1973), *The Mound Builders* (1975), *Serenading Louie* (1976), *5th of July* (1978), *Talley's Folly* (1980), and *Angels Fall* (1982), all directed by Marshall Mason. His other plays include *The Gingham Dog* (1966), *The Rimers of Eldritch* (1967), *Lemon Sky* (1969), and some twenty produced one-acts. He has also written the libretto for Lee Hoiby's opera of Tennessee Williams's *Summer and Smoke,* and two television plays, *Taxi!* and *The Migrants.*

Mr. Wilson received the 1980 Pulitzer Prize for Drama and the New York Drama Critics' Circle Award for *Talley's Folly.* Other awards include the New York Drama Critics' Circle Award, the Outer Critics' Circle Award and an Obie for *The Hot l Baltimore,* an Obie for *The Mound Builders,* and Tony award nominations for *Talley's Folly, 5th of July,* and *Angels Fall.* He is the recipient of the Brandeis University Creative Arts Award in Theatre Arts and the Institute of Arts and Letters Award.

Mr. Wilson makes his home in Sag Harbor, New York.